2/00

 St. Louis Community College

Forest Park
Florissant Valley
Meramec

Instructional Resources
St. Louis, Missouri

Voices of the Fugitives

A Ride for Liberty—The Fugitive Slaves. Eastman Johnson (1824–1906), circa 1862. The Brooklyn Museum. Gift of Miss Gwendolyn O.L. Conkling.

Voices of the Fugitives

Runaway Slave Stories and Their Fictions of Self-Creation

Sterling Lecater Bland, Jr.

Contributions in Afro-American and African Studies, Number 199

GREENWOOD PRESS
Westport, Connecticut • London

Library of Congress Cataloging-in-Publication Data

Bland, Sterling Lecater, date.
   Voices of the fugitives : runaway slave stories and their fictions of self-creation /
Sterling Lecater Bland, Jr.
     p.   cm.—(Contributions in Afro-American and African studies, ISSN 0069-9624 ; no. 199)
   Includes bibliographical references (p.) and index.
   ISBN 0–313–31169–2 (alk. paper)
   1. American prose literature—Afro-American authors—History and criticism.   2.
Fugitive slaves—United States—Biography—History and criticism.   3. American prose
literature—19th century—History and criticism.   4. American fiction—Afro-American
authors—History and criticism.   5. Slaves' writings, American—History and criticism.   6.
Identity (Psychology) in literature.   7. Passing (Identity) in literature.   8. Fugitive slaves in
literature.   9. Afro-Americans in literature.   10. Narration (Rhetoric)   11. Self in literature.
12. Autobiography.   I. Title.   II. Series.
PS366.A35 B64 2000
818′.30809896073—dc21   99–055223

British Library Cataloguing in Publication Data is available.

A paperback edition of *Voices of the Fugitives* is available from Praeger Publishers,
an imprint of Greenwood Publishing Group, Inc.
(ISBN 0–275–96707–7).

Library of Congress Catalog Card Number: 99–055223
ISBN: 0–313–31169–2
ISSN: 0069–9624

First published in 2000

Greenwood Press, 88 Post Road West, Westport, CT 06881
An imprint of Greenwood Publishing Group, Inc.
www.greenwood.com

Printed in the United States of America

The paper used in this book complies with the
Permanent Paper Standard issued by the National
Information Standards Organization (Z39.48–1984).

10 9 8 7 6 5 4 3 2 1

FOR MY PARENTS

ULA BLAND AND

STERLING LECATER BLAND, SR.

WELCOME TO THESE PAGES,

WITH LOVE AND THANKS

We rejoiced to hear of the fugitives' escape from bondage, tho' some of the pleasure was abridged by the caution to keep these things close. . . . Yes—publish his tale of woe, such narratives are greatly needed; let it come burning from his own lips in England and publish it here; it must do good. Names, dates, and facts will give additional credibility to it. Man and Many a tale of romantic horror can the slaves tell.

—Letter from Angelina Grimke
to Theodore Dwight Weld,
dated January 21, 1838

CONTENTS

ILLUSTRATIONS

Reading in the Breach

Reader, be assured this narrative is no fiction
—Harriet Jacobs, *Incidents in the
Life of a Slave Girl*

S TUDENTS initially entering the undergraduate classes I teach
on African-American literature are usually not surprised to see
slave narratives included on the reading list. Many are intrigued
by their inclusion. A small number have even had some experience
with texts like *Narrative of the Life of Frederick Douglass, An American
Slave* (most often in the context of history classes) or Harriet Jacobs's
Incidents in the Life of a Slave Girl (which they have usually encountered in women's studies classes). Most often, previous approaches had
sought to develop an understanding that primarily focused on the
overt political concerns addressed by the texts. Less frequently, the
emphasis had focused on a historical examination of the cultural importance of the narratives. But interpretive acts that rely exclusively
on one of these two methods (or even on some synthesis of the two)
are, to varying degrees, simultaneously clarifying and limiting.

Clearly then, this is a book that arises from a deep and sincere teach-
erly impulse on my part. As such, my aim is to direct my discussion
toward an audience that certainly contains specialists in African-
American literature but is not completely restricted to those readers.
To an extent, those well versed in the area may be somewhat familiar
with the basic outline of some of the concerns I raise. Rather, I am
particularly conscious of the need to develop in students, general readers, and those new to the field of African-American literature an
awareness of the characteristics and significance of the fugitive slave
narrative tradition. My purpose is to explore the ways slave narrators,
in the confluence of cultural and political contexts, sought to create
and authorize themselves and define their experiences. My task here is
to seek to engage both culture and politics in the service of language.

Initially, it all seems so clear to my students: Innocent people who were unjustly enslaved by a brutal system were getting to tell their own side of things, write their own stories. The stories recite the firsthand experiences of their narrators and indicate some of the substantial weaknesses in the fabric of American culture that many students see reflected in contemporary culture. Not surprisingly, many students find the narratives simultaneously compelling as moral allegories and thrilling as recitations of adventurous escape. In short, they respond as readers responded when the narratives were so in vogue in the decades immediately preceding the Civil War. They respond as readers of the narratives were intended to respond. There is a deep sense of romanticism, and a uniquely American romanticism at that, involved in hearing the story of someone struggling against seemingly insurmountable odds to achieve the morally sanctioned goals of human freedom and self-expression.

The instruction "Reader, be assured this narrative is no fiction," as Harriet Jacobs asserts in her narrative, is accepted by most in the class without question. Her narrative, like so many others, uses specific names and places and puts conversations within quotation marks to emphasize veracity. But is it really that clear-cut? That uncomplicated? Jacobs after all, I tell them, used pseudonyms. Douglass conflated experiences in his life into representative experiences. Was there maybe a larger design in the minds of the narrators? What role did the reading audience play in the process initiated by the narrator? The narrators had to tread a series of fine lines in which they understood themselves as both subject and object, self and other, author and narrative subject. In the relationship initiated by the existence of the narrative itself, there are no clear lines of distinction between these positions.

The breakdown of those boundaries extends to and implicates the reader also. As authors of their own stories, slave narrators brought relatively little power to their own text. One of the questions the reader is obliged to answer is how to discern the elements of authority that were made available to the narrator as the writer rhetorically created an identity. And given the relative lack of power the narrator possessed, how does our relative empowerment as readers change the ways in which the text is read and understood within contemporary culture? How does that subtle but important shift in the power arrangement change the ways in which the text even can be read? After all, the slave narrators themselves were deeply aware that their readers were intimately connected to their attempts at self-construction. And they were aware that telling the unvarnished "truth" about their lives paradoxically required a fictionalized element. The "truth" of their identities was not easily inserted into the rigid, two-dimensional form made available to them.

Given the inescapable involvement of the reader, how did narrators manipulate various fictions of self-creation for themselves? There needs, after all, to be some way adequately to acknowledge slave narratives as historical, politicized documents as well as to read the modes of creation they inscribe. I mean by that to suggest that slaves found it necessary to employ various masks and deceptions when obtaining their freedom. These masks are often reflected in a series of rhetorical methods of misdirection that ultimately open paths to insight and understanding for the reader. My aim is to attempt to construct a method of reading slave narratives that subordinates issues of "truth" to the issue of self-creation and the necessary fictions attached to that self-representation. It becomes clear that there are symbolic relationships that profoundly affect the ways in which ex-slave narrators constructed their stories.

My students are left with a newfound sense of instability concerning an area of writing they had initially found relatively certain and clear-cut. These narratives seem to promise a kind of verifiably authenticated truth. Instead, they raise a series of troubling questions about the connection between personal experiences and the ways in which these experiences can be reconstituted into a cohesive story. Seen in this light, the stakes become much higher for a group of students concerned with addressing the nebulous questions of identifying and defining black identity, of reconciling the importance of culturally instilling and maintaining a collective basis of shared African-American experience, and the considerable dangers inherent in failing to remember those experiences.

These students hope to construct a foundation upon which to place the basis of collective memory. They seek to find a literature appropriate for achieving that goal. Instead, they are forced to confront a body of writing that resists any attempts to classify it as a transcendentally objective solution to the problem. Rather, these stories pose as literary double agents that simultaneously manipulate the oppositional concerns I mentioned earlier.

My argument to my students is that for these texts, it is within the framework of doubling, mirroring, masking, and hybrid insubstantiality that their true significance lies. In the classroom, as I do here, I begin to search for meaning in the apparent breach between our expectations as readers and the "truth" these stories actually describe.

ACKNOWLEDGMENTS

I N WRITING this book, I enjoyed the intellectual companionship of many teachers, colleagues, students, friends, and family. I am extremely grateful for all of the contributions, both direct and indirect, they made to this project and to my development as a scholar.

I am grateful to James W. Tuttleton, Philip Brian Harper, Josephine Hendin, Cyrus R.K. Patel, and Kenneth Silverman for their guidance and suggestions. I have also benefited from the encouragement and inspiration of Arnold Rampersad and Donald Gibson.

A number of groups and organizations offered me the opportunity publicly to develop and rehearse my thoughts and ideas. The questions and discussion these presentations provoked helped me clarify and improve my thinking in numerous ways. These included the New Jersey State Museum; the Colloquium on Literature and Film, held at West Virginia University; work-in-progress colloquia held at Rutgers University and Princeton University; the South Orange Public Library; the South Atlantic Modern Language Association; Long Island University (Southampton); the International Conference on Borders and Foundations in Literature and the Visual Arts, held at West Georgia State University; the Newark Museum; New York College English Association; Towson State University Annual Multidisciplinary Conference on the Scholarship and Creativity of African Americans; Salve Regina University; and the Conference on Literature and Spirituality, held at Saint Xavier University.

I have had the luxury of thinking through some of the ideas contained in this book in various publications during the last several years. I gratefully acknowledge permission to reprint these essays here in revised and expanded form. These works include "The Unbearable Lightness of Boundary: *The Confessions of Nat Turner*," *The Journal of the Association for the Interdisciplinary Study of the Arts* 4 (Fall 1998): 55–65; and "Plain Truth and Narrative Design in Harriet Jacobs's *Incidents in the Life of a Slave Girl*," *CLA Journal* 43 (December 1999): 149–66.

The general and humanities reference librarians at Firestone Library at Princeton University and at Alexander Library, Mabel Smith Douglass Library, and Dana Library at Rutgers University made it possible for me to identify and locate the wide variety of materials I required to complete this project. I am particularly grateful to Mary George and Emily Belcher at Firestone Library for patiently offering assistance, guidance, and direction.

The community I have experienced while teaching and writing at Rutgers University in Newark, New Jersey, has made my work both enjoyable and intellectually stimulating. I am particularly grateful to Fran Bartkowski, Barbara Foley, Gabriel Miller, and Clement Price for being welcoming, encouraging about my work, and generous with their help. I would especially like to acknowledge the students who participated in the undergraduate "Introduction to African American Literature" classes I taught during the fall and spring semesters of 1996 and 1997 and the graduate seminar I taught during the spring semester of 1997. Their interest in African-American literature and their intellectual curiosity made my own explorations into finding ways to examine slave narrative writing fun, challenging, and exciting.

During the years in which the ideas for this book were formulated, given shape, and revised, I benefited from the stimulus, inspiration, and vision of teachers, fellow students, colleagues, friends, family, and acquaintances far too numerous to name. Several, however, deserve specific mention: David Carroll, Isabelle Kaminski, Marilyn Campbell, Jane Low, Alessandra Bocco, Jennifer Manlowe, Eileen Reilly, Julie Armstrong, Jacqueline Ivens, Toni Logue, Laurie Altman, Carolyn Fox, Freddie Belk, Edward Murray, Scott Murray, and Janice Bland.

Lastly, I would like to offer my deepest thanks and acknowledgment to my parents, Ula and Sterling Bland, Sr., for their unceasing love and constant encouragement. This book, which I hope they like, is lovingly dedicated to them both.

PART I

THE CALL . . . :

THE LITERARY AND

CULTURAL LANDSCAPE

Let the World Dream Otherwise:
The Literary Masks of Fugitive Slave Stories

> We wear the mask that grins and lies,
> It hides our cheeks and shades our eyes,—
> This debt we pay to human guile;
> With torn and bleeding hearts we smile,
> And mouth with myriad subtleties.
>
> Why should the world be otherwise,
> In counting all our tears and sighs?
> Nay, let them only see us, while
> We wear the mask.
>
> We smile, but, O great Christ, our cries
> To thee from tortured souls arise,
> We sing, but oh the clay is vile
> Beneath our feet, and long the mile;
> But let the world dream otherwise,
> We wear the mask!
> —Paul Laurence Dunbar,
> "We Wear the Mask" (1895)

SIMPLY PUT, this is a study of identity formation. I seek to address the techniques African-American slave narrative writers used to authorize and rhetorically create themselves in their writings. Some explicitly used Christian theology; some simply used religious language and its inherent values; others used the sentimental novel to authenticate their experiences and convey meaning; yet others sought to create authority for themselves by looking outward and calling into question traditional understandings of whiteness and blackness. Virtually all slave narratives employed masking strategies that were inscribed either in their language or their descriptions of experience. In short, all slave narrators engaged exterior structures in order to help them rhetorically authenticate themselves within the encircling confines of the fugitive slave narrative genre.

My intention here is to focus on the influential subgenre of the stories of those who had escaped slavery and had produced accounts of their experiences. They were frequently encouraged by (or, in the case of Nat Turner's story, in opposition to) literary sponsors. These sponsors were often involved with the antislavery movement. I emphasize throughout the importance of acknowledging and examining the decisions authors made in constructing their stories as a way of seeing how these stories influenced the discussion regarding the cultural context from which they arose.[1] Both the texture of the fugitive slave story and the relationship of the individual to the genre is admittedly broad. That texture serves to highlight the notion that assigning a specific value or worth to individual identity in a collective context ignores the fact that identity formation involves a series of processes of creation (self-creation, for instance, as well as cultural creation). In turn, these techniques often produce a series of identities that are somehow united to form the impression of a single, unique identity. There is an obvious correlation, of course, in the confluence of slave stories and those elements that facilitated their production. More often than not, the stories themselves sought to tell the literary relationship reflected by the power dynamics that characterized the slave experience.[2]

Though thoroughly grounded in the nineteenth century, fugitive slave stories adhere to and even transcend the postmodern aesthetic in the sense that they are ultimately not narratives about an individual self. Or about any self, for that matter. Rather, they are concerned with identity, especially black identity, as a cultural fabrication. Slave narratives became literary ghosts in a cultural machine that paradoxically made them completely fluid and fictional even as their authors and endorsers insisted upon their unvarnished truth. Another part of the power of the narratives, especially when they are seen collectively, stems from knowing that the reader is encountering (again, because of the pressures of the requirements of fugitive slave narrative production) essentially the same person in role after role. That role has a consistency and a core of personal integrity that underlies all writing that has any genuine claim to a reader's attention.

Having said that, it seems only fair to admit that my approach to that subject is informed by a series of interlocked assumptions. It is primarily based on the assumption that former slave narrators had to employ a variation of this kind of strategy because the fugitive slave narrative form was far too confining and two-dimensional to allow their writers to convey an adequate sense of themselves. It is also based on the idea that they saw the genre as being elastic enough to support various narrative strategies that were both complimentary and competing. Since the imposition of religious discursive elements, in either explicit or implicit fashion, recurs in so many ways in so many of the narratives, it seems both necessary and important to acknowledge the important function religious discourse plays in the ways some slave narrators grounded and explained their experiences.

The notion of grounding and explaining experience seems to provide a way of discovering "voice." Many of the literary critics who have examined slave narratives have mentioned the idea of "voice" or the finding of "voice," either through the acquisition of literacy, the physical act of ordering experience by writing the narrative, or through some combination of the two. This begs the question of why "voice" is such a recurring and important metaphor for the slave's experience and rhetorical representation of that experience. Employing the idea of "voice" allows for critical approaches that accommodate the doubleness and masking that are so often seen in relation to the black experience in America. But the idea of simply invoking a catch-all rubric like "voice" to stand in for distinctions that should be made between the individual and his or her collective sphere, between extratextual influence and authorial intention, and between the oral nature of the African-American folk tradition and the requirements and limitations of the literary narrative tradition is not as unproblematic as it appears.

The risk attached to using the metaphor of "voice" as a foundation and a point of extrapolation is substantial. Such a metaphoric practice takes from the narratives tensions encoded in the historical context of their production. As I will show, it also takes from them the transgressive appropriation of moral authority encoded in the various modes of authentication they employ. To argue for the idea of using the narratives simply as a way of seeing how slave narrators found their "voice" suggests a fragmentation and individualization of meaning and collective continuity that their rhetorical strategies argue against. An exploration of "voice" and vocal iteration, however, is crucial to an understanding of the slave narrative genre in general and to the relationship between the former slave narrator and his or her use of language. The very nature of the existence of slave narratives requires the awareness that they serve a variety of rhetorical, social, and political functions. Many of these capacities are played against each other in ways that ironically blur their lines of distinction. This may contribute to the difficulty and ongoing discussion literary critics have engaged in as they attempt to determine whether or not slave narratives should be considered autobiography, if they are more accurately investigated in terms of their uses as propaganda documents, or if there is some other rubric more appropriate for them.

At one rhetorical level, slave narratives were ostensibly stories of an individual unfairly and inhumanely enslaved. But the narratives served an autobiographical function that can be misleading. Slave narratives necessarily incorporate a first-person narrative structure that implies an autobiographical context. Yet, they should not be naively read as autobiography.[3] Furthermore, while the narratives make use of an autobiographical context to create a patina of veracity and accuracy, they are also very much the tools of a political agenda that is inherently different from, though intimately connected to, the autobiographical impulse. This is suggested by the "voices" placed at the margins of the narrative as well as by the "voices" that sometimes impose themselves on the narrative itself. In a representative example of the form like *A Narrative of the Adventures and Escape of Moses Roper* (1840), Roper's guarantor, the Reverend Thomas Price, writes on Roper's behalf that "His great ambition is to be qualified for usefulness amongst his own people; and the progress he has already made, justifies the belief, that, if the means of education can be secured for a short time longer, he will be eminently qualified to instruct the children of Africa in the truths of the gospel of Christ. He has drawn up the following narrative, partly with the hope of being assisted in this legitimate object, and partly to engage the sympathies of our countrymen on behalf of his oppressed brethren."[4]

Roper's narrative conveys a didactic intent that is assigned to it both from within and without. But Roper's narrative is not simply a monolithic, freestanding example of the autobiographical form. As with virtually all fugitive slave stories, it is forced to negotiate a series of tensions and oppositions. Roper's story is as much his own as it is the story of his "oppressed brethren," as much personal as it is political, and as much Christian as it is secular. Implicitly, there is a dialogue between Price's reluctantly authenticating introduction and the text of Roper's story itself. According to Price, another white abolitionist, the Reverend Dr. Morison, was originally intended to serve as Roper's guarantor. He fell ill and was unable to fulfill the duty, which was then passed along to Price. The recommendation of Roper's character had already been provided by someone identified only as an "eminent American abolitionist." This recommendor writes that " 'He [Roper] has spent about ten days in my house, . . . I have watched him attentively, and have no doubt that he is an excellent young man, that he possesses uncommon intelligence, sincere piety, and a strong desire to preach the Gospel. He can tell you his own story better than any one else; and I believe, that if he should receive an education, he would be able to counteract the false and wicked misrepresentations of American slavery, which are made in your country by our Priests and Levites who visit you.' "[5] Before the actual appearance of Roper's own "voice," then, that "voice" struggles against its very context for the opportunity to be heard and for control over the ways in which it might be heard and understood.

Henry Louis Gates, drawing on structuralist and Russian formalist thought, has referred to "binary oppositions," which he sees as being characterized by a series of qualities placed in relation to one another that encourages the reader to find meaning at the points of connection and disconnection. One of the drawbacks associated with this kind of oppositional paradigm is that it ultimately minimizes the complexity of the form. While slave narratives, with their emphasis on black and white or slave and free, strongly support this kind of binary reading, that paradigm should, at the very least, be modified to indicate that there are a series of binary paradigms at work. These must be simultaneously negotiated in all their uncertainty and ambiguity in order adequately to assess the subtlety of their meanings. My intention is to see the ways in which various kinds of double consciousnesses are reflected in many of the kinds of rhetorical doubling and masking that go on throughout slave narrative writing.[6] The doubling and masking employed by fugitive slave narrative writers as part of their authorial "voices" and rhetorical strategies include creating their identities out of the authorizing language of the Bible, rhetorically struggling for survival against the forces that ostensibly sought to liberate them, and even paradoxically masking their true intentions for freedom and escape behind the facade of compliance and acceptance.

The importance of illusion and masking in fugitive slave writing should not be diminished. Linda Brent, after all, creates the illusion to her obsessive master, Dr. Flint, that she has successfully escaped to the North while she lives for almost seven years in an attic crawlspace from which she is able to watch his comings and goings; Ellen Craft creates the dual illusion that she is both white and a man; and Frederick Douglass simply creates the impression that he is free and departs from southern bondage as a "free" man rather than a runaway slave.

I

The very opening of W.E.B. Du Bois's *Souls of Black Folk* (1903), his meditation on race, black identity in the United States, and the "strange meaning of being black," indicates both the origins and definitions of his notions of "doubleness" when he writes that "Between me and the other world there is ever an unasked question."[7] As Du Bois frames it, that unasked question, namely "How does it feel to be a problem?," is usually circumscribed within other seemingly less highly charged questions. Yet the question remains. And the modes of response to that question are defined by the "vast veil"[8] that separates black experience and identity from the larger body of American identities.

As Du Bois explains it, his initial awareness of the separation occurred when the white classmates in his New England school decided to exchange visiting cards. His card was refused without consideration by a newcomer to the school: "The exchange was merry, till one girl, a tall newcomer, refused my card,—refused it peremptorily, with a glance. Then it dawned upon me with a certain suddenness that I was different from the others; or like, mayhap, in heart and life and longing, but shut out from their world by a vast veil." Thus, Du Bois's composition of "doubleness" is founded upon the socially constructed gaze, depicted by the disparaging glance of Du Bois's classmate. That gaze creates an artificial division between white and black that obscures more fundamental similarities of thought and aspiration.

As truncated and elided as is the exterior gaze, Du Bois's formulation suggests that the interior gaze is similarly fractured and disfigured. African Americans are limited by the exterior manifestation of social response and are thus able only to see themselves and be seen "through the revelation of the other world."[9] It would therefore appear obvious that any true representation of African-American identity in this social context must require the engagement of that "other world." The engagement of the "other world" is crucial to the creation of a black self because that self is so strongly formed by the assumptions and interpretations of that world.

But Du Bois also suggests that the "doubleness" that is created between black and white and separated by a veil is also reflected by a "doubleness" within the ways in which black identity can be culturally established. Thus, when Du Bois writes that "[T]he Negro is a sort of seventh son, born with a veil, and gifted with second-sight in this American world,—a world which yields him no true self-consciousness, but only lets him see himself through the revelation of the other world,"[10] Du Bois suggests a culturally inscribed boundary that allows African Americans the ability to see beyond the veil and use the power of "second sight" to see both what is in front of and what is shielded by the veil.

In *The Alchemy of Race and Rights* (1991), Patricia Williams offers a personal account of experience that similarly emphasizes the disparity between vision, mirroring, and the social ideologies that align self-presentation with visually judged, performative aspects of identity:

Buzzers are big in New York City. Favored particularly by smaller stores and boutiques, merchants throughout the city have installed them as screening devices to reduce the incidence of robbery: if the face at the door looks desirable, the buzzer is pressed and the door is unlocked. If the face at the door is undesirable, the door stays locked. Predictably, the issue of undesirability has revealed itself to be a racial determination. . . . I discovered them and their meaning one Saturday in 1986. I was shopping in SoHo and saw in a store window a sweater that I wanted to buy for my mother. I pressed my round brown face to the window and my finger to the buzzer, seeking admittance. A narrow-eyed, white teenager wearing running shoes and feasting on bubble gum glared out, evaluating me for signs that would pit me against the limits of his social understanding. After about five seconds, he mouthed "We're closed," and blew pink rubber at me. It was two Saturdays before Christmas, at one o'clock in the afternoon; there were several white people in the store who appeared to be shopping for things for *their* mothers.

For Williams, the social implications of vision are clear. Vision allows the person employing the gaze to make a series of claims about the object of the gaze. The disjuncture, of course, is that the person wielding the gaze makes a series of intuitive leaps between what is seen and what cannot be seen. Furthermore, according to Williams's experience and the fact that the door she faced remained locked, knowing the "truth" of whether or not one is correct in arriving at the conclusions one has is immaterial. One can rely on this kind of visual method of investigation to make blanket decisions about who is or who is not a member of the community with which one identifies (and is therefore desirable or undesirable). For the person wielding the gaze, this is most important. Williams continues:

> I often wonder if the violence, the exclusionary hatred, is equally apparent in the repeated public urgings that blacks understand the buzzer system by putting themselves in the shoes of white storeowners—that, in effect, blacks look into the mirror of frightened white faces for the reality of their undesirability; and that then blacks would "just as surely conclude that [they] would not let [themselves] in under similar circumstances."[11]

Both Du Bois's and Williams's experiences (temporally separated by almost 100 years) with race and their interpretations of race and socially constructed identity are significant both proactively and retroactively. In the context of my reading of fugitive slave narrative writing, they constitute an especially useful theoretical starting point because of their emphasis on the ways in which African Americans must be actively aware of the socially constructed parameters within which they exist as individuals. By extension, their rhetorical constructions of themselves reflect this awareness.

There is a struggle for African-American existence in this rhetorical context that is also suggested by the mediated nature of the texts themselves and by the masking strategies the slave writers used to give their texts meaning. But the texts themselves are often divided against themselves. They struggle to exert their own "voice" against the annihilating rhetoric of their white guarantors. Many of the narratives show that there is a sense of internal conflict and "doubleness" that is as powerful as what happens outside the veil. Thus, Du Bois's assertion that "One ever feels his two-ness,—an American, a Negro; two souls, two thoughts, two unreconciled strivings; two warring ideals in one dark body, whose dogged strength alone keeps it from being torn asunder"[12] defines the serial nature of oppositional qualities inherent in the formation of African-American identity.

But there is a paradox here. Du Bois almost seems to be arguing that given the "doubleness" inherent in a social system that grants full or partial citizenship on the basis of race, these "warring ideals" can never be fully resolved for African-Americans. Indeed, it is the clash of ideals that defines for Du Bois the African American experience: "The history of the American Negro is the history of this strife,—this longing to attain self-conscious manhood, to merge his double self into a better and truer self. In this merging he wishes neither of the older selves to be lost. He would not Africanize America, for America has too much to teach the world and Africa. He would not bleach his Negro soul in a flood of white Americanism, for he knows that Negro blood has a message for the world. He simply wishes to make it possible for a man to be both a Negro and an American, without being cursed and spit upon by his fellows, without having the doors of Opportunity closed roughly in his face."[13] So how then, especially in the case of a slave narrator, is an African-American writer supposed adequately and convincingly to create a rhetorical space appropriate for consumption by a white readership while simultaneously juggling the clash of both external and internal assumption? How is one to negotiate in a cultural context so delineated by social expectation and, ultimately, race? My assertion throughout this study is that fugitive slave narrative writers almost universally employed various rhetorical masking devices, especially in direct or indirect relation to the authorizing power of biblical precedent and literary and cultural expectations based on race, gender, and class that allowed them to engage both the internal and external aspects of that conflict.

II

When Paul Laurence Dunbar writes in his poem "We Wear the Mask" (1895) that "With torn and bleeding hearts we smile, / And mouth with myriad subtleties," he unites the ideas of masking and language. These suggest the ways slave narrative writers sought to render their stories with the various masking and obscuring strategies that occurred within those stories. Like Du Bois, Dunbar's poem suggests the kind of fracturing that happens on both sides of the mask. But Du Bois is also aware of the internal division that this external division causes; and paradoxically enough, Du Bois is able to see a beneficial effect, which he refers to as being "gifted with second-sight in this

American world."[14] The benefit of that gift is that blacks may be said to have a view of the world on the other side of the veil that allows the possibility of transcending the socially inscribed conditions of the outer world upon which they gaze.[15]

The tension generated in fugitive slave narratives usually centers on the method of escape. This is especially true since readers knew by the very existence of the narrative itself that the narrator had successfully escaped. The use of masks and disguises became a commonplace component of the genre. What makes the slave narrative run, at least in the narrator's telling of the story (as opposed to the framing devices), is the how of the escape. Hazel Carby's comments about Pauline Hopkins's *Hagar's Daughter* (1901) that "Conventional use of disguise and double identities indicated a disruption of the natural order of events, whereas the revelations and resolutions of popular fiction signaled the reestablishment of order in the moral and social fabric of the characters' lives" are also relevant to slave narratives. The doubleness and deception the narrators were forced to internalize and employ also represented a fundamental flaw in the American body politic.[16]

These deceptions take on additional meanings when viewed in relation to Du Bois's "double-consciousness" or Bakhtin's theory of "double-voiced discourse." The deceptive acts described in the narratives are mirrored in rhetorical "voicings" that are profoundly aware of the circumstances existing on both sides of the veil. In his book *Harlem Renaissance* (1971), Nathan Huggins notes that "The stereotype—the mask—defined the Afro-American as white Americans chose to see him; outside the mask the black man was either invisible or threatening. Negroes, accepting the pretense, wore the mask to move in and out of the white world with safety and profit."[17] Though limited in their modes of response, slave narrators saw both the limitation and possibility encoded in the mask and turned themselves into rhetorical trickster figures who appropriated various modes of storytelling in ways that both masked and gave resonance and moral weight to their narratives.

The historical approach I have chosen to use emphasizes a very specific sociopolitical phase of American history to which other studies have alluded. My purpose is to contribute a reading of fugitive slave narrative writing that examines in some detail the production of these narratives in direct relation to religious, rhetorical, and social influences and constraints from which they arose. I intend to argue that the various kinds of doubling inscribed in slave narrative writing were

an imaginative and creative (as well as an honest and accurate) response to the contradictions inherent in a supposedly Christian nation
that tolerated the slave system. I have attempted to go beyond the
obvious kinds of correspondences that are possible in a study that by
its own definition attempts to cross the boundaries between literary
criticism and historical context and look instead toward the reasons
for and tensions between generic conventions and the impulses that
created them. My intention is to trace the relationship between rhetoric and social ideology in order to see how that relationship was manipulated within this specific literary genre. And the fugitive slave narrative genre, from its origins in New England antislavery activity in the
1830s through its extraordinary popularity in the years preceding the
Civil War, was an extremely specific, though influential, genre.
Though it had an extraordinary influence on subsequent writing like
Herman Melville's "Benito Cereno," James Weldon Johnson's *Autobiography of an Ex-Coloured Man*, Richard Wright's *Black Boy*, Ralph
Ellison's *Invisible Man*, William Styron's *The Confessions of Nat
Turner,* Sherley Anne Williams's *Dessa Rose*, Charles Johnson's *Middle
Passage*, and Toni Morrison's *Beloved*, the slave narrative should not
be seen as the only outlet for black writing before the Civil War. This is
especially true since not all antebellum African Americans were slaves.
Furthermore, as I will discuss a bit later, the particulars of the genre
offered men far greater opportunities to tell their stories than women.

Slave narratives (accounts of experience written by slaves or former
slaves) form a large percentage of all published writings by blacks in
the United States before the Civil War. The fugitive slave narrative
(those accounts of slavery and eventual, often adventurous, escape
North) is a smaller portion of the larger slave narrative genre. It has
received, and continues to receive, a large proportion of critical attention. This is primarily because of the opportunities fugitive slave stories offer to examine, in close proximity, the interplay of "voices" and
influences. The narrators negotiated the murky, ill-defined influences
contained in stereotype, competing interests in how the narratives
should be used, and particularly the rhetorical strategies fugitive slave
narrators used. These rhetorical strategies are especially significant in
light of the impersonal way slave writers often used language in the
depiction of their experiences. Unlike the larger genre of slave narrative writing, the fugitive slave subgenre allows for the opportunity to
gain some insight into the cycle of "double voicings" inherent in black
experience and reflected in its written representation. While virtually

all fugitive narrators at least make mention of the importance of literacy and the barriers attached to attaining that literacy, it is the act of writing their experiences from their newly acquired positions of relative freedom (or, in the case of Nat Turner, his position as an escaped fugitive who was subsequently captured and whose story is presented as a kind of legal deposition) that most emphatically highlight the series of "double voicings" they describe.

III

Moving back and forth between literary production and the contexts specific to that production (that is, between examinations of language and social power) is not new to critical thought. Neither is the idea of asserting these concepts in relation to African-American writing. The fact that fugitive slave narrative writers fail to transcend the effects of power and influence against which they struggle does nothing to extinguish their relevancy and interest. With these ideas in mind, though, I have sought as my objective to use particular texts to illustrate the individual and collective ways narrative writers accommodated, resisted, and refined the generic literary options made available to them. This strategy of moving between historical context and textual representation seems especially useful as a critical tool because the conditions in which the texts were produced are virtually inseparable from the very composition and rhetorical strategies the texts themselves employ. Examining fugitive slave narratives generically, with an emphasis on the factors encoded in specific aspects of their production, provides an opportunity to examine the ways specific texts functioned in the establishment of the genre. It also provides an opportunity to examine the ways individual texts worked in concert with and in opposition to the characteristics of that genre.[18]

Each of the narratives I will examine is explicitly concerned with creating an individual literary "voice" out of the memory and recollection of experience. Complicating the reader's awareness of this creation of literary "voice" is the mediating presence of others who involve themselves with the narrative and whose comments often frame (and sometimes interrupt and intrude upon) the slave's narrative. Since these "voices," usually in the form of introductions, endorsements and appended documents, are integral to the reader's awareness of the depth and power of the slave's story, the slave narrative becomes a strongly mediated form, further conflicted by the dual role it is forced to perform. It is simultaneously a literary document of personal expression and a political document designed and manipulated by others, often abolitionists, in support of their own agenda.

I see this study as an attempt to reconfigure and resituate what is now a generally accepted truism concerning mediation. I hope to develop a culturally based narrative theory that locates the slave narrative within the context of contemporary views of nineteenth-century literary history and narrative theory, and acknowledges the complexity of the slave narrative form. The success of the slave's narrative is a function of the narrator's ability to create a common human bond between reader and narrator, while simultaneously emphasizing the horrors and brutality associated with an inhumane slave system. In connection with this notion of extraliterary mediation, one of the crucial issues I explore is the question of the slave's relation to his or her own narrative. In connection to that, it is important to examine how narrators rhetorically authorize themselves and how narrators reconcile themselves to the moral boundaries imposed by the culture.

These general interests and assumptions form the basis of my approach in this study. But the African-American fugitive slave story is too complex a mode to understand by an examination based solely on these kinds of generalized criteria. Arising from these general questions and assumptions are deeper, more compelling questions that demand examination: When I speak of the "fugitive slave narrative," I am referring to a first-person narrative that makes self-conscious use of a literary aesthetic. But is the writer's self-conscious use of a literary aesthetic indeed present? And, if so, in what form does it appear? Does any particular style of storytelling or narrative discourse characterize the narratives? Any particular structure? What roles does memory play in the narratives? What relationship and influence do the mediator and the audience exert over the creative impulse of the ex-slave who now writes his or her narrative? What relationship do slave narratives have to each other? What are the variations involved in the creation of "voice" between different narratives? Or different narratives written by the same author, as in the case of Frederick Douglass? Or even in a single narrative in which the slave's "voice" is so very connected to the "voice" authorizing that narrative that at times it is virtually impossible to separate the former slave's "voice" from the editor's "voice," as in the case of Nat Turner's *Confessions*. Based on this, is it possible to make any general claims for regarding the writing of the slave narrative as a creative act? Are these claims adequate in explaining the creation and development of an African-American literary mode? How can the slave narrative be located within the context of nineteenth-century literary history or twentieth-century theories of race, gender, and identity?

It is especially difficult to examine African-American women's fugitive narrative writing from this period because of the relative shortage of texts available for review. This is partially because in the same way as society rarely provided nineteenth-century women, black or white, with opportunities to express their literary talents, black women were sought out to tell their stories proportionately less (and themselves sought less public attention) than their male counterparts.[19] But black women's writing reflects the same kinds of issues that occur in the writing of black men. Slave narratives written by both men and women tend to emphasize mental, physical, or spiritual bondage (or some combination of the three) that is represented by a narrative plan depicting the narrator's attempts to free himself or herself from this kind of confinement.[20] But black women add to this tradition their own position as black women living in a society that judged them on their gender as well as their blackness. As one would expect, African-American women's fugitive narrative writing used and redefined many of the slave narrative forms that were available to male African-American writers.

Women, black and white, in the nineteenth century were encouraged to pursue ideals of domesticity and submission. These aspirations are reflected, to varying degrees, in an emphasis on domestic and spiritual values. In many of the narratives of escape written by men, the emphasis is on adventure and the intrigue of escape from slavery. Many women's narratives (like Harriet Jacobs's) alter the perception that all black fugitive slave narratives are stories dominated by male protagonists that adhere fairly narrowly to a particular form. Of course, the overwhelming majority are male dominated stories and do adhere to the fugitive slave narrative form that was so strongly encouraged by the white antislavery movement, publishers, and its reading audience.

Several elements may have contributed to the attitudes black women encountered as they, like speakers such as Frederick Douglass and William Wells Brown, sought to find their "voice" on the antislavery platform. There was a constant possibility of physical reprisal of audiences hostile to their words. There was also a bias against women speaking in public or even publishing their ideas in antislavery publications. The public sphere assumed, on behalf of the speaker, an authority and resonance that was traditionally ascribed to ministers. It is therefore not surprising that a great deal of the criticism leveled (initially, at least) at women public speakers was from those discomforted by the apparent threat to their authority. Interestingly enough, there is also a class-based barrier to former slave women speaking on their own behalf. A noteworthy number of black women speaking in public came from free black families who had been able to provide education and societal standing that many former slave speakers like Sojourner Truth and Ellen Craft did not possess.[21]

IV

Though many literatures, fiction and nonfiction, are deeply influenced by the social contexts from which they arise, black fugitive narrative writing is especially sensitive to the religious, political, artistic, and social forces that inform it. By appropriating various literary techniques, African-American fugitive slave stories sometimes take on characteristics of fiction. Hence the oft-repeated phrase (or some variation of it) in the prefatory material of fugitive slave narratives asserting that the following narrative is "true" and underrepresents rather than exaggerates the experiences of the narrator. Black narrative writers invariably cross the boundaries between fictional writing, sermons, jeremiads, philosophical writing, and political writing in presenting an individual and cultural self. Similarly, my analysis stretches beyond the rigid confines of literary analysis in an effort to recognize and engage the historical and social components embedded in the texts.[22]

In keeping with the call and response relationship of culture and African-American writing, the first portion of the book, "The Call," examines in some detail the context of the cultural and literary models at work. In the second portion of the book, "The Response," I turn to close readings of selected narratives. The narratives I have chosen offer a series of points of comparison. They also, individually and collectively, provide divergences from the context of narrative style from which they arise. My reading of these texts involves engaging them (in what is often an uneasy balance) on the level of what they say about the narrator (a level that is simultaneously autobiographical and self-authorizing) and in terms of how they engage, contradict, and otherwise amend other texts.

In the course of this study, only Nat Turner's *Confessions* almost unilaterally falls beyond virtually all of the accepted boundaries of the fugitive slave narrative. Turner was not a fugitive narrator in the same sense that Douglass, Jacobs, or William and Ellen Craft were fugitives. His was not an escape North and therefore did not employ the oppositional qualities assumed by the other narrators. Though his text mediates black experiences for white readers, the audience served by Thomas R. Gray's composition of the text was undoubtedly hostile to that experience. Furthermore, it is often unclear throughout the work (even in the portion that purports to be verbatim testimony) where Gray's "voice" ends and Turner's begins. But Turner's *Confessions* is very much a part of the paradigm I have created for the fugitive slave narrative in spite of, if not because of, many of these exact qualities.

On the basis of these lines of thinking, Chapter One offers an evaluation of the rhetorical moment in which these slave stories were produced. I begin by examining language and its relationship to the development of African-American literary expression in the larger context of American assumptions about African Americans and their experiences. This begs the question of exactly what are those assumptions and how are thoughts on African-American experience reconciled within the amorphous, reciprocal engagement of a multiracial cultural environment. Compelling arguments can (and have) been made on behalf of the claim that African-American writers have long had a presence in American literature and culture.[23] My aim in constructing this initial chapter the way I have is to acknowledge that presence while focusing on the stories narrators told and the identities they embroidered out of what amounts to little more than literary and cultural "found materials." Within these "found materials," there remains a fundamental imbalance of power. I argue that this has as much to do with the boundaries circumscribing black narrators as it does with who gains (or retains) interpretive control over the text.

Part of the difficulty one faces in addressing the interpretive aspects of these stories is that they have traditionally been seen in strict relation to the particular experiences they describe. They have not been examined in terms of the kinds of forms and structures they must successfully manipulate and engage in order to authorize and substantiate a literary presence that was otherwise suspect. There are a series of narratological correspondences centering around the conditions and inherent limitations of memory and self-creation as it relates to autobiographical writing. Part of the dilemma facing former slaves who had escaped slavery is that the literary rehearsal of their experience was so much a function of their social and political moment. Individuals were often subsumed into a collective explanation of what slavery itself was "really like." In seeking to achieve this objective of presenting objective, verifiable incidents, slave narrators assigned an arbitrary beginning and end to their experiences and, by extension, an arbitrary series of values and meanings that could adequately authenticate those experiences.

Chapter Two examines what is clearly (and in so many different ways) the most problematic text of all those discussed here. Nat Turner was most certainly a fugitive slave and his story is an outgrowth of those circumstances. But that is where the most obvious points of comparison end. Turner's escape was to a field near his home at the Travis farm, not to the North; Turner defines his actions in relation to an oppositional disparity between the sacred and the secular rather than to more commonly used distinctions between slave and free or South and North; furthermore, Turner's amanuensis was obviously hostile rather than sympathetic to his story. Yet even with all of its apparent limitations, the text's qualified status highlights many of the difficulties contained in the genre.

I have already addressed the understanding that the fugitive slave story is, at best, strongly influenced. In Turner's story, the lines of influence and collaboration are obscured to the point that it becomes virtually impossible for the reader to fully separate Turner's "voice" from that of his amanuensis, Thomas R. Gray. But in attempting to devise a form substantial enough to contain Turner's story, Gray uses a series of smaller components. They ultimately form a structure inadequate fully to achieve his stated objective of trying "to understand the origin and progress of this dreadful conspiracy, and the motives which influence its diabolical actors" (*CNT* 40).

One of the most terrifying aspects of Turner's insurrection for white southerners was the fact that even up to the last moments preceding his uprising, Turner and his co-conspirators wore a mask of docility and acceptance that fully obscured their actual intentions. But the structural configuration of the text, a legal-style deposition (though not an actual court deposition) framed by a series of Gray's contextualizing documents, only serves to emphasize and look toward the kinds of masking and rhetorical sleights-of-hand that characterize other fugitive slave stories. In a genre emphasizing absolute, unvarnished truth, Turner's *Confessions* exposes a clash of intentions and rhetorical techniques that renders objective certainty, or even complete certainty about whose story the reader is supposed to accept, impossible adequately to judge.

Chapter Three examines the ways Frederick Douglass fabricates and establishes himself in *Narrative of the Life of Frederick Douglass* (1845) by engaging religious language and biblical precedent. The very structure of the *Narrative* emphasizes the revival-style antislavery convention at which William Lloyd Garrison "discovers" Douglass's strength as a public speaker and at which Douglass himself claims to have initially discovered his "voice." But as I argue, Douglass's *Narrative* transcends the boundaries of a sermonically inspired critique of slavery and becomes instead Douglass's self-defining rendering of the complex relationship he perceives between himself, the slave community, and their relationships (sometimes complimentary and sometimes antagonistic) to American culture.

Ultimately, the *Narrative* serves to create an understanding of "voice" that is as much individual as it is the product of its intersubjective arrangement within its cultural moment. Though seemingly haunted by a need to address and resolve the question of origins, Douglass can offer very few of his own. He does not truly know who his father is (though the accepted suspicion is that his master is his father). His mother comes to him literally hidden in the darkness of night and figuratively obscured by the recollections culled from Douglass's earliest childhood memories. In the central area of the *Narrative* (his battle with Edward Covey and the providential appearance of Sandy Jenkins and his talismanic root, which was clearly derived from African religious belief), Douglass creates a meaning for himself that engages, though hardly defines or absorbs for himself, all of these indeterminately disparate elements.

Chapter Four addresses the related issues of authority and rhetorical ownership as they are addressed in Douglass's *My Bondage and My Freedom* (1855) and Harriet Jacobs's *Incidents in the Life of a Slave Girl* (1861). Whereas Douglass's earlier *Narrative* was overtly concerned with his attempts to authorize his "voice," *My Bondage and My Freedom* reorients that "voice" within the context of the tensions inherent in becoming a public figure. *My Bondage and My Freedom* encircles and interprets the earlier *Narrative* in the same way the earlier *Narrative* is encircled and interpreted by Garrison's antislavery rhetoric. One of Douglass's deepest realizations in *My Bondage and My Freedom* is of the stereotyped roles blacks were expected to fulfill by slaveholding southerners and antislave northerners alike. Douglass's response to these stereotyped roles is constantly to reorient his individuality to a larger black community and to assert the interpretive component that he comes to see as the true basis of authority.

One of the difficulties inherent in Douglass's expanded formulation of himself is that he became a freeman whose only option was to define himself in the context of his status as a former slave. The concentrically circular form of *My Bondage and My Freedom* suggests for Douglass a double act of creation that ultimately finds fulfillment outside of either of the earlier narratives and instead in the establishment of his own newspaper the *North Star*. Having his own newspaper offered Douglass the possibility of a self-constructed platform unrestricted by the generic constraints of the fugitive slave story. Clearly, though, even that "voice" was defined by the boundaries inscribing African-American social and rhetorical constructions of "voice."

In *Incidents in the Life of a Slave Girl*, Harriet Jacobs faced the difficulty of framing and authorizing her story in a way that allowed that story to be her own while simultaneously engaging socially prescribed views of womanhood. The realities of that rhetorical product risked censure on a number of fronts. Whereas Douglass ultimately arrives at a decision to separate his narrative "voice" from his narrative subject by founding the *North Star*, Jacobs's decision to use pseudonyms and her intentional blurring of "fact" and "fiction" achieves a similar goal. In a subtle but important deception, Jacobs has managed rhetorically to construct an engaged distance between herself as the person who has experienced and written the narrative and the protagonist of that narrative. In a similar mode of fragmentation involving the reader, Jacobs has created an implied audience within the text that differs from but mirrors the actual reader. In many ways, the rhetorical space that Jacobs creates for herself is as boundaried and mediated by the narratee as Turner's text is mediated and confined by Thomas R. Gray. The antislave system that encouraged other male writers to tell their stories was too narrow for Jacobs to tell her own story.

For Jacobs, the emphasis on objective, verifiable facts was subordinate to the self-referential control of her own words. This intratextual, self-referential component was extremely important for her because textual references to and assumptions about the reader indicate Jacobs's awareness that her ideal reader could never fully understand the text itself or the difficulties Jacobs encountered as she composed it. Ultimately, the narrative gains its authority by situating itself in an area that continually struggles against dissolution. After all, the narrator, Linda Brent, in her various asides to an idealized reader, is clearly aware that she can never fully convey the depth of her experiences. Her reader is inadequately prepared to understand a story that resides beyond the socially dictated roles of marriage and motherhood expected for women. Since, for Jacobs, the politics of difference outweigh areas of commonality between her and her reader, these categories cannot fully absorb the cultural weight placed upon them when they refer to slave girls. Hence, the narrative's authorizing elements are a function of Jacobs's ability rhetorically to expose the tactics of oppression commonly employed by the South (silence, shame, and physical and psychological limitation) and expand the parameters of that analysis to a larger discussion of black female coercion based on silence and rhetorical control.

Chapter Five examines *Running a Thousand Miles for Freedom; or the Escape of William and Ellen Craft from Slavery* (1860) in terms of the ways the Crafts seek to define a narrative authority for themselves by questioning and reworking traditional arrangements of race, gender, and class. The Crafts use these categories as a way of subverting commonly held social views about the meaning and significance of those categories. To a large extent, nineteenth-century America was predicated on a very narrow and fixed set of oppositional social conceptions: black and white, male and female, gentleman class and laboring class. In their narrative, the Crafts articulate and exploit an awareness of the fluid indeterminancy that describes social identities. The narrative is driven by an intricate masquerade in which a black slave woman successfully impersonates a white slaveholding man. Ellen and William Craft initiate their escape based on a series of conjectures that require the reader to make a succession of conceptual realignments about the relationship of whiteness to blackness, masculinity to femininity, and mastery to slavery. Furthermore, Ellen's act of passing means that the definition of identity no longer suggests a transcendent, essentialized, fixed quality.

The implication, though, is that whiteness itself came under the scrutiny of a black subject intent on showing the ways in which whiteness was performative. The reader of their narrative is given access to both sides of the performance: The self-identity and the socially constructed version of that identity. And paradoxically enough, it is the black author of the narrative who brings the concept of whiteness forward for the inspection of the reader. In many ways, *Running a Thousand Miles for Freedom* is very much a narrative about readers and reading. The success of the ruse depends on the "readers" who encounter Ellen in her disguise unquestioningly to "read" her in terms of what she appears to be. Since Ellen cannot speak, lest she give herself away, William, in his ability to describe the experience, creates for himself a certain level of rhetorical authority.

1

Dismantling the Master's House:
The Cultural Context

There was neither voice, nor hearing
—II Kings 4: 31

[T]he master's tools will never dismantle
the master's house.
—Audre Lorde

I N TERMS of literary origins, all things begin with language. Language expresses internal emotions and describes external experiences. In most situations, language must be adapted and shaped for individual expression. In "Discourse in the Novel," Mikhail Bakhtin notes that "Language, for the individual consciousness, lies in the borderline between oneself and the other. The word in language is half someone else's. It becomes 'one's own' only when the speaker populates it with his own intention, his own accent, when he appropriates the word, adapting it to his own semantic and expressive intention."[1] Richard Wright, in *12 Million Black Voices* expresses a similar sentiment when he writes of stealing "words from the grudging lips of the Lords of the Land" and modifying those words until "although they were the words of the Lords of the Land, they became our words, our language."[2]

Language preceded the arrival of the first African slaves to Jamestown, Virginia, in 1619. But language, especially as applied to the status of blacks, has virtually always involved a dual purpose. By taking from slaves their native languages and imposing a new language upon them, slaves were forced to reconcile their own inexpressible conceptions of themselves with the versions of their identities that were reflected to them through the conceptions of others. Rhetorical structures in the form of speeches, sermons, pamphlets, and books defended and justified the slave system.

Words, as Richard Wright correctly notes in *Black Boy*, can indeed be used as weapons. But they can also be used as a form of defense. Though their sense of cultural identity had been taken away, black writers/narrators worked to gain control over the rhetorical representations that defined their experiences and identities in America.[3] The notion of examining the fugitive slave narrative as a particular subgenre is, by extension, a way of discussing the larger body of African-American literary expression and the relation of that expression to the unfolding of African-American culture. The definition of that culture, as well as the examination of its traditions, is as complex and problematic as defining the literature that grew out of it.

The master and slave relationship that Shakespeare presents in *The Tempest* has significant implications for the ways in which American slavery and its connection to language can be approached. One of the things that inscribes the boundary between masters and slaves is who has access to language and, more importantly, who actively interprets the language and creates its meaning. In the case of the slave, the appropriation of language and the establishment of meaning provided an opportunity for the slave to subvert and redefine those things to which he or she had linguistically been given access.[4]

Prospero graciously offers Caliban, his "savage and deformed slave," the gift of his language:

> When thou didst not, savage,
> Know thine own meaning, but wouldst gabble like
> A thing most brutish, I endowed thy purposes
> With words that made them known. But thy vile race,
> Though thou didst learn, had that in't which good natures
> Could not abide to be with. Therefore wast thou
> Deservedly confined into this rock, who hadst
> Deserved more than a prison.
>
> (*The Tempest*, I. ii. 357–64)

The danger contained in Prospero's "gift" to Caliban is that it so clearly places Caliban's expression of his experience in a position in which that expression can only be seen through the mediating "voice" of Prospero's conceptions of himself. This suggests Edward Said's thoughts on "orientalism," in which certain groups are defined as "other" within the context of western thought. But in my reading of this passage, I am suggesting that the master-slave relationship, inasmuch as language is concerned, is unique because it does not simply reinforce the cultural dynamics of hegemony. The master-slave relationship demands for itself the ability to place slavery's subjective qualities within the context of the master's language. That language is then informed by all the racially inspired doctrines inherent in colonizing discourse.[5]

The implications for this study of this reading of the master-slave relationship are clear: The African-American presence in fugitive slave stories has relatively little to do with a literary agenda concerned with portraying individual experience. It has much more to do with reducing the slave narrator to an abstraction whose function was to mirror the climate in which he or she was restricted. As Toni Morrison argues, "[I]f the language of ones culture is lost or surrendered, one may be forced to describe culture in the language of the rescuing one. . . . Under such circumstances it is not just easy to speak the master's language, it is necessary."[6] The possibilities of the former slave writer enduring within the house constructed by the master's tools are, at best, deeply jeopardized. At worst, the art of rhetorically creating a self is virtually made impossible by the need to use outside authorizing strategies that reaffirm blackness as something other than the self. That effectively creates a discrete, separate container of African-American experience reconfigured for a white audience in terms that audience could understand.

Although the slave appropriated language, that appropriation was tempered by the slave's very status as a slave. Prospero and Caliban have access to the same language, but there is a potency to Prospero's words (the master's words) that is not fully reflected in Caliban's use of language. At one point, Caliban seems unwilling to carry out Prospero's command and Prospero threatens him by saying:

> If thou neglect'st, or dost unwillingly
> What I command, I'll rack thee with old cramps,
> Fill all thy bones with aches, make thee roar,
> That beasts shall tremble at thy din.
>
> (*The Tempest*, I. ii. 370–73)

Caliban realizes Prospero's ability to carry out his threat and responds accordingly:

> I must obey: his Art is of such pow'r,
> It would control my dam's god, Setebos,
> And make a vassal of him.
>
> (*The Tempest*, I. ii. 373–76)

Eventually, though, slaves appropriated the language and its power by shaping the language with their own meanings.[7]

Black American writing is closely shaped and defined by the culture from which it arose. The imprint of cultural influence on black writing is nowhere more apparent than in slave narratives. That influence should not draw attention away from the ways in which narrators have sought to form narrative identities. They synthesized and challenged already existing American forms and meanings with methods of storytelling particular to their own interpretation of their experience. Literary and cultural encapsulation contained within it the tools of authorization and self-creation.[8]

Examining black culture in the context of its commodified relationship to American culture has a great deal in common with the ways former slave writers used language and the ways in which that use of language (that is, the narratives themselves) was commodified in the marketplace. There is an inherent "double-voicing" in this kind of relationship. The marketplace effectively reduces everything to its lowest common denominator by making everything intrinsically similar. Most slave narratives (and certainly the majority of antislavery-sponsored narratives by runaway slaves) bear more than a casual resemblance to each other. That similarity may be seen as reflecting the capacity of the marketplace subtly to divest slave narratives of the particular in favor of the most abstract, generalized characterization of "slave."

As a commodity, the former slave's story was used by antislave organizations (or, in the case of Turner's narrative, by Thomas R. Gray) with the intention of achieving their own political goals. The narrator occupied the problematic position of being a commodified intermediary between the "seller" of the narrative and its prospective buyer. Thus, the uniformity of perceptions about what was perceived as a homogeneous group conveniently contained in the designation "slave" places the narrator in a peculiar position. Linguistic acquisition and appropriation must be somehow authorized from outside of the narrator's experiences as a way of differentiating the individual beyond the commodified representation of the individual.[9]

The earliest black writing in America used the forms available to it, including the Native-American captivity narrative, the sermon, the jeremiad, the spiritual conversion narrative, and the narrative of self-advancement. Later, with the growth of the abolitionist movement in the 1830s, black writing was channeled in the direction of the fugitive slave narrative form. This mode was itself a literary formulation synthesized from a political need to have former slaves narrate their experiences of slavery and escape for northern white audiences eager for true stories of action and adventurous escape against monumental odds. The genre became so popular during the height of antislavery activity (approximately 1830–1865) that current estimates place the number of slave narratives (including published narratives and unpublished manuscripts) at approximately 6,000. An article entitled "Black Letters; or Uncle Tom Foolery in Literature," which appeared in the February 1853 issue of *Graham's Illustrated Magazine of Literature, Romance, Art, and Fashion*, bewailed the volumes and volumes of what it referred to as the "literary nigritudes" [sic] flowing from publishers such that "shelves of booksellers groan under the weight of Sambo's woes, done up in covers! . . . A plague on all black faces! We hate this niggerism, and hope it may be done away with . . . If we are threatened with any more negro stories—here goes. . . . In the name of the Prophet—not the bookseller's profit!—let us have done with this wooly-headed literature; let us have a change; let us have a reaction. . . . We are really weary of preaching negroes."[10]

I

Throughout African-American literature, and the majority of antebellum black writing, there is an emphasis on society and the relation between society and the individual. A great deal of attention is given to teaching white readers about the lives and experiences particular to blacks. Taken together, these characteristics have been problematic to the ways African-American literature has been read and evaluated. For example, it has been assumed that writing about African-American culture and society has been too specific in its focus to speak toward and comment upon the kinds of issues that pervade the fabric of society. In short, they are perceived as lacking the ability to stand outside of their historical time. The very nature of the slave narrative compels an understanding of the social circumstances that shaped and defined the genre. But many of the slave narratives themselves, especially among the narratives written during the eighteenth century, seek to universalize their message by obscuring specific references to race and slavery and instead focus on elements like religious conversion or high adventure.[11] To truly understand the poignancy of African-

American writing in general, and antebellum fugitive slave writing in particular, it must be read in light of the social and cultural contexts that give it meaning.[12]

Even examining the genre in the context of these expanded, amorphous boundaries severely minimizes a number of important elements, the most important of which is the function and use of memory. The narratives are written at a time in which the narrator, through conscious manipulation of memory, is looking back over the experiences of a life and actively shaping those memories in a way that provides meaning and coherence. These slave narratives are considerably more than a chronological outline of experience. Though clearly rooted in an historical and cultural moment, they also transcend the particularity of that moment by combining the literary present with the experiential past in a way that creates a system of meaning and correspondence. The very act of recollecting, organizing, and writing about the human condition serves to create a literature that extends beyond the limitations of strict narrative reconstructions bound by historical context. Slave narratives have traditionally been seen in relation to the experiences they describe and not in relation to the creative processes that produce them. The sense of form and structure they create is often overlooked in favor of the reality they describe. By developing out of the memory and recollection of a shared African-American experience, the slave narratives describe a reality that is simultaneously individual and collective.

But what of this simultaneous relationship between the individual and the collective? African-American writers have historically been seen as being bounded by the limitations of describing individual experience within the context of a larger social setting. Since society is constantly changing, individual black experiences have not been seen as universal enough to illuminate the human experience. A critical approach to literature that emphasizes form, structure, and those features suggestive of more universal, nontemporal elements jeopardizes the understanding of a great deal of African-American literature. It especially endangers the comprehension of the slave narrative, whose very existence implies that the social and cultural realities present in the daily lives of slaves take precedence over the literary appropriation of some kind of transcendent, universal standard.

The voices comprising slave narrative writing present a recurring sense that although the tale is framed as a story of individual experience, the reader is actually listening to an individual "voice" that subtly represents the experiences of the entire race. Individual consciousness is so much a function of collective experience that to discuss one without the other is pointless and ultimately counterproductive to the work of attempting to understand a collection of literature that is consistently inscribed as deeply by the social and the political as it is by the individual. In so many ways, former slave writers produced, predictably enough, a body of writing patterned by their allies and the requirements of their audience. The most unsympathetic reading of these elements argues for what seems to be a misguidedly romanticist belief in the eventual assimilation of white and black cultures.[13]

As I have noted earlier, the imprint of influence and mediation is everywhere apparent in African-American writing, arguably more so in the slave narratives than in any subsequent African-American mode of literary expression. But this should not be taken to mean that black history and culture were fully assimilated and made invisible. Elements associated with black history and culture transformed and were transformed by the social settings from which they grew. The willingness of black writers to use literature as other than a form of social protest is very much a function of the awareness of both blacks and whites of the power of literature to define and change society. It reinforces the understanding that black writers themselves mediated and explained to whites the experiences, perspectives, and aspirations of blacks.

II

The discussion of slave narrative writing requires some discussion of autobiography as a genre. The autobiographical mode serves as a way of arriving at a fuller understanding of what I mean by "slave narrative" and how that rubric is distinguished from the "fugitive slave narrative" subgenre, which this book takes as its subject. Autobiography assumes various forms, including the memoir and the diary. For the uses of this study, autobiography refers to a style of writing in which the writer, from a particular place in life, looks back over a lifetime of experience and writes about it in hopes of finding in that experience some sense of coherence and meaning.[14] Seeing autobiography in this way allows readers of slave narratives to see them in ways that acknowledge the variousness of their origins while also recognizing the correspondences that connect the narratives. This is not to

suggest that slave narrative writing, especially stories published between 1830 and 1865, when the fugitive slave narrative was particularly prevalent, is not remarkably homogeneous in its structure and
approach.

Eighteenth-century slave narratives exhibit a variousness of structure, tone, and intent that stylistically sets them apart from their nineteenth-century counterparts. But they share with the later narratives,
as well as with virtually all formulations of autobiography, an emphasis
on memory and recollection that highlights the distance between
the actions being recounted and the artistic act of reconfiguring
those experiences. All autobiographers are selective in the experiences
they recollect and in their selection of experiences from those recollections. They give the impression that a particular narrative is intended
to be completely comprehensive. Autobiographical writing is intended to chart a path of meaning and relevance, which is very different from being simply an unexamined record of experience. In other
words, there may be a large disparity between the configuration of
the autobiography and the actual events of the life. Autobiography is
not necessarily untruthful or otherwise unreliable, but the composi-
tional elements inherent in writing autobiography preclude an ency-
clopedic approach to life-writing. Autobiography highlights and emphasizes elements that are perceived by the writer to be significant in
his or her life.

In his article entitled "Using the Testimony of Ex-Slaves: Approaches and Problems," which was originally published in 1975,
John W. Blassingame's use of the word "testimony" in referring to
the stories of former slaves is especially prescient when seen in relation
to contemporary politicized movements.[15] These movements equate
silence with death. Memory becomes synonymous with a cultural
duty intended to hold individuals and societies accountable for their
crimes, which are construed as either active participation or a passive
unwillingness adequately to confront the wrongdoing of others. Contemporary culture has become obsessed with testimony, as indicated
by real and cyberspace obsessions with celebrity court cases and the
proliferation of television talk shows that mimic true testimony. They
allow in-studio engagement and out-of-studio meta-engagement by
those viewing the shows. The performance of the autobiographical
artifact has become such that testimony is now a central characteristic
encoded in the ways contemporary culture engages with and makes
sense of its cultural moment. Given this context, the rubric of autobi-

ography and its goals need to be reconfigured to accommodate the ways individual experience can profitably be used in the service of endorsing a larger conceptual discussion. And this, to me, is exactly what fugitive slave narratives are consistently called upon to do. They, as a rule, contain preciously few details concerning the personal histories of the narrators. Instead, these narrators must create themselves out of an insubstantial and unsubstantiated historical basis. That act of rhetorical creation is necessarily as resistant to autobiography as it is accepting of the forms and conventions of autobiography.

The masks adapted by former slave narrators are actually the distorted images of themselves presented them by their culture. Paradoxically, in seeking to tell their stories, their audiences were forced to confront the same stereotyped images they themselves helped create and nurture. In this context, the notion of testimony supersedes any notions of autobiography because the testimony of those who have experienced the crime firsthand implicitly forces the burden of the problem into the hands of the reader. The speaker of the narrative has come forward to bear witness to that which he or she has seen and experienced. Though the reader will not be called upon to offer testimony, he or she is metaphorically called upon to offer judgment.[16]

The literary shaping and creative involvement of the writer is especially apparent in autobiographical cycles like Frederick Douglass's *Narrative of the Life of Frederick Douglass, an American Slave* (1845), *My Bondage and My Freedom* (1855), and *Life and Times of Frederick Douglass* (1881). Brilliantly rendered scenes from the first narrative are subsequently altered and subtly revised in ways that indicate that Douglass, over the course of his life, discovered new meanings—or at least interpreted the old meanings in new ways. As his memory of the events changed, so did his understanding of the significance of those events. But fugitive slave autobiographers differ from many other kinds of autobiographers because explicit in their narratives is a desire to persuade. This is one of the difficulties inherent in discussing fugitive slave narratives as being either particularly autobiographical or literary in intent. The malignant pervasiveness of the slave system is constantly presented as threatening to extinguish the individual spirit. Therefore, the autobiography becomes less a biography of the self and more a discussion of the overlap of social forces and individual life.

From one vantage point, the fugitive slave narrative illuminates the individual by the ways in which the writer chooses to render the clash between the personal and the political. But it is the political, a recurrent and unavoidable theme throughout fugitive slave narratives, that is foregrounded. The individual is often a metaphor of the collective, further complicating the understanding of the autobiographical imperative. The rather narrowly drawn desire to reconstruct the experiences of an individual life is less useful here than it might be in other forms of autobiographical writing because individual life is routinely depicted as being a product of the political atmosphere. This form of life-writing should not be separated from other more accepted forms of autobiography. The writing of ex-slaves does everything one would expect to find in "standard" autobiographies. That is, the slave narrators use their memories to find in their experiences a sense of meaning and texture. Through the act of writing a narrative based on phases and events of a life, they create a dialogue between the personal and the political, and the individual and the collective.

To a large extent, any autobiographer runs the risk of overstructuring, and therefore oversimplifying, his or her experiences. By virtue of the process of memory and the selective process of composition, areas of connection mistakenly appear continuous, logical, and over-determined. Certainly, the narrative's outcome trespasses on the narrator's rehearsal of the events he or she describes.[17] Furthermore, the slave narrator, particularly the writer of the fugitive slave story, had several problems to overcome in order to ensure the proper reception of the narrative. Since the narratives were largely directed toward a northern white audience, there was inherently a certain amount of suspicion and distrust on the part of a reader about the narrative "voice."

Even the earliest examples of black narrative, like the documents containing court records of *Adam Negro's Tryall* (1700), appear in close connection to abolitionist publications, like Samuel Sewall's *The Selling of Joseph* (1701). As this connection became stronger in the early nineteenth century, a series of literary conventions were imposed on black writers by the abolitionists who encouraged the production of slave narratives for their own political purposes. James Olney is correct in noting that "The lives in the narratives are never, or almost never, there for themselves and for their own intrinsic, unique interest but nearly always in their capacity as illustrations of what slavery is really like. Thus in one sense the narrative lives of the ex-slaves were as much possessed and used by the abolitionists as their actual lives had been by slaveholders."[18]

In a literary sense, slave narrators are further faced with the structural problem of having the outcome of their experiences inform the presentation of the experience itself. Their end is in their beginning. The very existence of the narrative indicated the successful nature of the escape.[19] Unlike other autobiographical forms, fugitive slave narratives all focused on the same goals: The depiction of an individual life in relation to the social and political culture that controlled virtually all its aspects, and the creation by the narrator of an appreciation in his or her readers of the inhumane conditions of black life in America, in hopes of ending the slave system.[20] Furthermore, black writers and their literary sponsors had very specific audiences they hoped to persuade. Slave narrators wrote as an act of rebellion, but a rebellion deeply informed by the relationship between writer, literary sponsor, and intended audience in which the slave narrator was required to mediate experience and politics.

One of the narrative strategies employed to achieve these goals was to use the journey motif as a way of rhetorically creating a sense of order and progression that probably did not otherwise exist. The journey could take the form of a spiritual journey, a picaresque journey of action and adventure, or, in the case of fugitive slave narratives, a literal journey from South to North. This sense of journey underscored the sense of distance most African Americans felt from virtually all social practices and associations—whether familial, geographic location, or financial stability—that usually provide a sense of order and security. It is this sense of separation and disenfranchisement that ultimately creates the tone that informs African-American autobiographical writing, whether written by Equiano Olaudah, Frederick Douglass, Harriet Jacobs, or twentieth-century writers like Richard Wright or Maya Angelou.

Throughout slave narrative writing, there is a sense of tacit reliance on what, for lack of a better phrase, can best be described as the American Dream. There is a sense of optimism and possibility that, like the existence of African-American writing in general, seems closely connected to the antislavery agenda. The irony of slave narrators relying so heavily on the journey (or escape) motif is that the fugitive slave narrative form did not embody the sense of expanse and possibility it suggests. Slave narratives are ultimately confining even in escape because the identity they create is so publicly defined. Their discovery of "voice" is compromised by the fact that their rhetorical creation of identity was based on a series of fictions ascribed to them by the public arena.[21]

The narratives absorbed the beliefs of Christian theology, as well as the ideals of enlightened thinking and constitutional ideals. There was an implicit belief that conditions for black Americans would ultimately improve. And the belief was that the escape from slavery initiated this process. Present conditions did not guarantee a spiritual or political transcendence. But implicit within black narrative writing is the sense that with a few modifications, the system could be refined in such a way that everyone would be equally represented. In short, there is a distinct movement toward the development of a black middle-class aesthetic, represented by the sense of movement between an ambiguous faith in American political and social institutions and a genuine faith in the notion of some kind of transcendent American Dream that would ultimately encompass blacks as well as whites in elevating the quality of life for all in America. These ideas of possibility were largely transmitted to blacks through the efforts of the abolitionist movement and Protestant Christian doctrine.

I am arguing here for a conception of autobiography that recognizes it, however much the function of a certain amount of self-creation and outright fiction, as basically the "narrative of a person's life written by himself."[22] There are instances in slave narrative writing where fictional forms mirror the autobiographical forms. Books like *Uncle Tom's Cabin* (1851) by Harriet Beecher Stowe reflect the ways sentimental fiction of the period was influenced by the literary cross-racial dialogue, while books like Richard Hildreth's *The Slave; or Memoirs of Archy Moore* (1836), *Jamie Parker, the Fugitive* (1851) by Emily Catherine Pierson, *The Autobiography of a Female Slave* (1857), written by Martha Griffiths Brown, and *The Martyrs, and the Fugitive* (1859), written by the Reverend S. H. Platt, are examples of fictionalized autobiographies that used the slave narrative technique in hopes of capitalizing on the popularity of the genre. Ironically, some of these fictionalized accounts of the slave experience, especially *Uncle Tom's Cabin*, had a large influence on public attitudes regarding slavery.[23]

In each instance, the autobiographical form has been coopted in order metaphorically to create a life reflective of the cultural circumstances through which the narrator has lived. But autobiography itself seeks to realize these same objectives. In so doing, autobiography blurs the distinctions of technique that are usually associated with fiction writing and "factual" writing. The province of autobiography itself is intrinsically unclear. In order to write the story of a life, the individual is essentially looking back over certain episodes and arranging them (in a sense, initiating a literary phenomenon in the conscious writing of that life) into an artificial rhetorical structure. That structure locates the life and its experiences within a particular cultural framework. There is an imaginative, nonfactual component implicit in the autobiographical form that catapults it away from the factual confines of history and into the imaginative preserves of literary art.

The autobiographical form in general and the fugitive slave story in particular suffer from the problems inherent in a form that requires the writer rhetorically to construct a useable past from the viewpoint of the present. The "design and truth" assessment of autobiography seems to presuppose a strategy in the construction of autobiography that eliminates any artistic inflection or intention.[24] For many writers of autobiography, there is an uneasiness between the text that is developed from the constraints of the narrative "design." The created text is necessarily selective in the kinds of detail it can adequately present. Even if a writer wished to write a comprehensive autobiography, some incidents and occurrences would necessarily either be emphasized or backgrounded in favor of the narrative demands of the text. But rather than simply being a strict presentation of fact, the details of the narrator's life are revealed within the framework of an aesthetic setting that intentionally guides the reader toward the understanding the narrator has of his or her experiences.

One thing that distinguishes the slave narrative from other autobiographical forms is the confluence of cultural and political elements with the spirit of self-expression and social rebellion. The writer's imaginative spirit rests unnoticed though clearly visible among the forest of narratological characteristics that claim the attention of the reader.[25] But one of the difficulties of writing what is essentially an historical narrative is that history confounds any attempt to assign a particular beginning and ending. Many writers of autobiography encounter a similar arbitrariness as they assign value and meaning to their experiences. For the fugitive slave narrator, there is a built-in conclusion because the tension of the narrative strategy usually centers around the desire to achieve some kind of freedom. Once this freedom has been achieved, the impetus of the narrative ceases. But in order to create a reason for the reader to view the narrator as a sympathetic figure, the narrator must first present himself or herself as a character within the framework of a highly stylized sequence of events. Clearly, the main character (and writer of the narrative) does not perish during the course of the story, but is able rhetorically to create a sense of pattern and movement whose meaning becomes revealed as the implicit design of the narrative becomes clear.

By telling the story of both what happened and what did not happen, the slave narrator uses a factual, easily documented setting to express a story of individual experience that has collective ramifications. While exercising a certain amount of license in form and structure, the slave narrator is able to impose an interpretation upon the progression of events that he or she is obliged faithfully to sketch. Here the fugitive slave narrative genre begins to separate itself from the already amorphous body of narrative and autobiographical writing from which it emerges. There is a didactic voice common to all fugitive slave narrative writing that makes it clear that the manipulation of various structural components works toward specific narrative objectives.[26]

Literature commonly placed within the boundaries of what is termed "autobiography" varies a great deal in the kinds of experiences it incorporates. St. Augustine's *Confessions* are theological explorations as much as they are discussions of an individual life. Or rather, they are the discussion of a life in terms of the spiritual events the writer saw as shaping his life. Similarly, *The Education of Henry Adams* is the discussion of a life in terms of an intellectual history. Henry David Thoreau's *Walden* offers as much insight into how one can create a well-lived life as it does into the intricacies of Thoreau's conception of his own life. Rousseau's *Confessions* attempt to reach some sense of understanding about the self. Unlike each of these autobiographies, different as they are in form, structure, and intent, the slave narrator desires to use the elements of autobiography to create a story whose value is rooted in the fact that it is the narrative of a former slave. He or she tells a story based on the creation of patterns of episodes that are intended to make a dramatic point regarding slavery. This kind of narrative seeks to use the effects of fiction by incorporating many of the resources usually associated with the fiction writer, such as plot, characterization, episodic structure, and dialogue.[27]

In being transformed by and transforming the narrative strategies available to them, African-American narrators recast the narrative conventions in terms comparable to the ways Rousseau transformed the confessional form. Rousseau wrote openly about sexuality in a way that defended his actions and sought fairness in judgment instead of writing a confession like Augustine, who recorded a life of debauchery coupled with eventual salvation. In talking about the events of his public life in his *Autobiography*, Benjamin Franklin did not limit himself to a strict presentation of his public self. He managed to talk about it in a way that incorporated his private wants and desires and their relation to his public persona.

With the tradition of the confession centering on the interior life of the individual and the tradition of the memoir centering on public life, the slave narrative forms the point of convergence between the interior and the exterior as well as the point at which history and fact is connected to literary imagination. When slave writers composed their narratives, they usually included the dates when the experiences occurred as well as the approximate time in their lives when they were writing. The temporal realities of the narrative are not cast merely as parenthetic biographical details but as a way of authenticating the text. By describing their lives in terms of temporal reality as well as in terms of politics, culture, and religious and social conditions, African-American writers were able rhetorically to create themselves in terms of a specific point in American history.[28]

Having said all of this regarding the distinctions between autobiography and narrative, I must stress that speaking about the antebellum African-American narrative involves a problematic distinction. All narratives that fall within the boundaries of either slave narrative or fugitive slave narrative do not necessarily achieve or attempt to achieve similar levels of personal reflection or self-exposition. In many of the narratives, the reader learns surprisingly little about the inner life of the writer beyond his or her thoughts on slavery. It is as if a veil is drawn or a mask put on to separate the innermost thoughts of the black writer from his or her audience. Though so much a part of the narrative and so important to its successful reception, the "voice" of the individual is often concealed in the surrounding form and structure.

The first-person narratives I discussed earlier were specifically written with the intention of rhetorically finding meaning and structure within an individual life. In the slave narratives, this is rarely the case. The narrative uses the individual life to provide to northern whites a depiction of the slave system. Put differently, virtually all slave narratives used individual lives to look outward rather than inward to thoughts and motivations. This is especially true when those thoughts and motivations pertained to issues other than slavery. In so many respects, the narrative form was confined to a very specific parameter fairly strictly defined by the desires and objectives of abolitionists and the audiences to whom they wrote. And in some ways, the very form of the narrative itself paradoxically negated the presence of the individual even as it purported to tell his or her story.[29]

PART II

. . . AND THE RESPONSE:

SPEAKING FOR THEMSELVES

2

Religion, Revolt, and the Commodification of Language: The Limitations of "Voice" in *The Confessions of Nat Turner*

Testify v. (1840s–1990s) to confess one's sins, bad deeds, life
story (originally in church but now in music, in literature,
and through other forms of art); to ritually comment upon
any cultural experience understood by all black people; a
secular or religious confession. . . . Example: "I want to
testify this evening to the goodness of my Lord and to the
fact he directed me away from a life of sin."
—*Juba to Jive: The Dictionary of
African-American Slang*

T HE *Confessions of Nat Turner* (1831) is, in so many ways, a
resistant text. A great deal of that resistance is caused by the
rhetorical blurring of boundaries that characterizes the text.
It invokes religious conversion as a primary thematic and structural
element, yet it is not a conversion narrative. Similarly, it defies categorization as slave narrative, autobiography, or even jailhouse confession.
Because of the way it varies from actual court transcripts, it resists
categorization as a reliable representation of either history or the legal
process. A text that begins with the promise of unmasking the motivations and objectives of a group of slave insurgents ends with their
leader's silence. The story of Thomas R. Gray, who seeks to soothe the
public mind after the insurrection, concludes by consigning Turner to
the role of religious fanatic, thus forestalling any serious discussion
about the contributing role played by the institution of slavery.

So what exactly does a reader see? One of the keys to a deeper understanding of the text is an awareness of the fact that the text is read
backward. By that I mean that the reader knows the conclusion of the
story at the outset. The narrative is intended to provide the details

leading to that conclusion. The reader, after all, knows from the very beginning that "The insurgent slaves had all been destroyed, or apprehended, tried and executed, (with the exception of the leader)."[1] The premise of the text, as posed in Gray's introduction "To the Public," makes it clear that Nat Turner had been captured and had agreed before his execution to offer some explanation concerning "the motives which governed them, or the means by which they expected to accomplish their object" (*CNT* 40).

The text seems to promise a sequential disclosure of the "history of the motives which induced" (*CNT* 44) Turner to undertake the insurrection. It delivers both a history of Turner's own spiritual development and an example of the way Gray's distortion of the facts surrounding the incident reveals as much about Gray and his agenda as it does about Turner. Because of Gray's agenda and the control he takes over Turner's story, the *Confessions* is not the best source for learning about Nat Turner.[2] Ultimately, out of the fragmented, double-voiced textual construction that takes place between Nat Turner and Thomas R. Gray, the final narrative, taken as a whole, presents Nat Turner's "voice" in such a way that, even within the context of his own story, the boundaries of that "voice" are finally obscured to the point that it struggles against Gray's for its own rhetorical existence. My objective in this chapter is to examine the ways in which the collapse of textual boundaries that comprise the text creates a hybrid document in which Nat Turner's "voice" is often indistinguishable from Thomas R. Gray's. The meaning and significance of the story is therefore created in the conflict and confluence of "voices" the story incorporates.

Gray says in his preface that his objective in compiling and publishing Turner's "confession" is to explain the reasons for Turner's decision to enact his rebellion and to soothe public fears of a large-scale slave rebellion. But unlike other slave stories in which the form and structure of the narrative mean that the individual "voice" of the narrator disappears as the narrative serves to universalize black experience, Nat Turner's narrative works against that model. Rather than allowing the individual voice of his narrative to be subsumed in any kind of collective reading of his experience, Turner completely individualizes himself by refuting the possibility of any collective explanation. The beginning of Turner's section of the narrative is in apparent response to a question Gray has posed, asking that Turner offer an explanation for a history of the motives that prompted the Southampton insurrection. Gray attempts to elicit from Turner an explanation that will place the events surrounding the present reality of the insurrection in the most general, easily historicized terms possible. Turner rejects this opportunity and instead places the origins for the insurrection in the most particular, individualized terms available to him. Gray's master narrative becomes an attempt to define a sense of order and coherence between Turner's personal experience and the public expression of that personal experience.

The ultimate suggestion, though, in Gray's inability to arrive at a coherently rendered authoritative "voice" suggests that a monolithic, authorizing master narrative is ultimately impossible to create. Instead, the "history" that Gray requests from Turner (and that Gray himself seeks to challenge) can only be fulfilled within the context of a series of micro-narratives that often not only compete against each other but are sometimes even in direct contradiction to each other. Turner's narrative itself, with its intense semiotic scrutiny of natural phenomena, suggests a progression of signs and symbols that to Gray and his readers bear no resemblance to the truths those signs and symbols should describe.

Turner becomes, for Gray, a truly postmodern subject. The fragmentation and apparent lack of semiotic coherence that Turner displays via Gray's creation of the *Confessions* takes from Gray the possibility of a historicized context. This, after all, is what he requests of Turner. Instead, that historicized element is replaced with a highly personal logic and interpretation that ultimately grants Turner a power and authority that has nothing to do with Gray and everything to do with the parameters within which Turner has defined himself. The irony is that in order rhetorically to create himself, Turner appropriates a language (traditional Protestant Christian discourse) that, in and of itself, is not his own. Yet Turner makes it so that that language is his own by interpreting the images connected to that language. He essentially refutes Gray's interpretation, which sees him as being ideologically fragmented and untethered. To the contrary, Turner casts himself in strongly authorizing terms. The point of concern for Gray and for Gray's reading audience is that Turner's rehearsal of the thoughts and experiences leading up to the insurrection bear no apparent relation to their interpretation and understanding of those terms. For them, the insurrection was wholly and completely without foundation.

The notion of an interpretative discontinuity—a semiotic difference—is almost a truism regarding this text. The tensions between the diametrically opposed worldviews of Gray and Turner are, after all, at the very heart of the narrative. What is not as apparent is the way in which Gray, in an apparent reversal of appropriation, turns Turner's text into a commodity intended to argue against the very possibility of southern cultural breakdown the rebellion itself suggested. If Turner's section of the *Confessions* is interpreted by Gray in an attempt to fragment and disconnect Turner's actions from any larger slave plot of rebellion and even from any larger framework of thought within Turner himself, the *Confessions* as a whole suggests on Gray's part the desire for completeness.

"Be it remembered," the very first words of the prefatory material to the work from the district clerk, imply collective memory. Similarly, at the opening of Gray's "Notice to the Public," he notes that this open rebellion is the first of its kind "in our history" (*CNT* 40). But the collective memory into which Nat Turner is placed is not a rhetorical memory. It is a memory based upon his actions. The final act of rhetorical interpretation belongs to Gray, against whose contextual landscape the circumstances of the *Confessions* are placed. Turner's actions, as Turner himself may have understood when he agreed to be interviewed by Gray, required a rhetorical setting in which to gain meaning. Eric Sundquist suggests that Gray needed Turner as much as Turner needed Gray and that, due to the lessening of his financial fortunes after being disinherited by his father, Gray's need to commodify Turner was substantial.[3] This, I believe, is largely true. What is additionally true is the fact that virtually all who read the signs and symbols connected to the larger "text" that Turner represents (that is, his actions, the resulting narrative, and the exterior reactions to that narrative within a collective framework of cultural experience) found it possible to use Turner for their own agendas. And this is partially made possible because of the fragmented, micro-narratives that Gray uses to compose the text.

I

Even Garrisonian abolitionists appropriated, for their own agendas, Nat Turner as a kind of demonic figure ultimately representative of the kind of violence lurking beneath the facade of southern tranquillity. Fundamentally, the antislavery movement viewed slavery as sin and sought to bring about its abolition on Christian and moral grounds. But within these boundaries was also the abolitionist's insistent belief that the slave system would eventually lead to a race war that threatened to devour all who stood in its path: "A cry of horror, a cry of revenge will go up to heaven in the darkness of midnight, and reecho from every cloud. Blood will flow like water—the blood of guilty men, and of innocent women and children."[4] Garrison's position, as outlined in a speech he gave on July 4, 1829, was the combination of religious and social consciousness that applied evangelical religious doctrines to the issue of slavery.

Through the reform movement, Garrison and his followers saw an opportunity to respond to the use of evangelical faith that Lyman Beecher, the father of writer Harriet Beecher Stowe, and other likeminded ministers like Charles Gradison Finney and Nathaniel Taylor preached. Beecher taught that people could bring about their salvation by abandoning sin and embracing a benevolent life. Basically, the antislavery movement used religious language as the controlling metaphor for its work in the same ways slave writers like Nat Turner took and transformed religious language for their own uses. In a letter to *The Liberator*, a woman wrote: "Four years ago the Lord delivered my spirit from all parties, and socialties, of whatever name and object; and I have not since recognized myself accountable to any but my Heavenly Father."[5] Individual conscience alone was to be used as a guide, rather than adherence to a particular political or religious affiliation. Garrison expressed his benevolence through his antislavery reform activities and through his writings in *The Liberator*. A great deal of his antislavery argument rested on constant recitations on the immorality of slavery and on a growing awareness that slave rebellion was not only possible but probable.

Garrison's anxieties were confirmed with the publication of David Walker's *Appeal* in late 1829 and with Turner's subsequent 1831 revolt. As he watched the elements leading to slave rebellion becoming more and more apparent throughout the American psyche, he and his followers became more fearful of the possibility of slave violence: "We do not preach rebellion, no, but submission and peace."[6] Garrison seemed to hold to the possibility of a nonviolent solution to the issue of slavery. Because of this, *The Liberator* was especially critical of Walker's *Appeal* because it called on slaves to use violence, if necessary, to achieve their freedom. The review appearing in the May 14, 1831, issue of *The Liberator* revealed an acute awareness of the growing potential for slave rebellion and rightfully saw the need only for someone to step forward and lead that rebellion:

Negroes have showed their mental capacity in St. Domingo, where, thirty-two years ago, they were as much or more debased that they are now in the United States. That example of bloodshed and misery is before the eyes of our slaves; that tragedy, it seems to me, will soon be enacted on an American stage, with new scenery, unless something is especially done to prevent it. The actors are studying their parts, and there will be more such prompters as Walker. *At present, they only want a manager.*[7]

The prophesy of this manager, one who sanctioned his activities with biblical allusion, appropriated the apocalyptic language of the New Testament, and inverted its meaning so that it endorsed and supported the activities of black revolutionaries, was fulfilled in the appearance of Nat Turner, who initiated his insurrection about three months after the appearance of this review of Walker's *Appeal*.

Turner's *Confessions* presents a moral reading of life soundly based in religious language. Turner presents himself as a prophet rebelling against an immoral system and embarking on a kind of holy war against the white people who maintained and upheld the slave system. His family were slaves in the household of Benjamin Turner, who had become Methodist some time during the late 1780s or 1790s. At the time, the Methodists had separated from the Anglican Church and begun to expand on the doctrines of free will and independent salvation preached by the Anglicans. Methodist revivalists initially preached against slaveholding, though not with the same sense of conviction as, for instance, the Quakers. Most southern whites were fairly unwilling to free their slaves, who represented status to them. Slavery furthermore provided them with a way of maintaining control over the large numbers of blacks throughout the South.

By early in the nineteenth century, the Methodist church had officially backed away from this stance and had chosen instead to accept the doctrine of slavery in places where slavery already legally existed. As a bit of a compromise, Methodists chose to allow members to own slaves, but not actively to engage in buying and selling them. Methodist ministers were not allowed to have slaves at all. After a while, even the rule against the buying and selling of slaves was relaxed and the church instead focused its attention on the need to Christianize the slaves in an effort to ensure their salvation. As with most of the Christianity taught to slaves, the emphasis was placed on present salvation and the need to accept salvation in preparation for an afterlife of happiness. Following these beliefs, the Turners held prayer meetings on their farm for their slaves and regularly took their slaves to church with them on Sundays.[8]

Nat Turner was born in 1800 and even as a child by all accounts seemed especially intelligent. He was encouraged to learn to read so he could study the Bible. But because of the kind of precarious existence described throughout slave narrative writing, Nat's life was changed when he was nine years old. His father unexpectedly ran away, leaving his wife and children behind. Nat's master died and Nat was willed to his master's son. His new master was as religious as his father, but also a bit sterner. This master's use of Christianity was more in line with the thinking of slaveholders throughout the antebellum South. For him, Christianity was as much a tool for salvation and deliverance as it was a tool for maintaining obedient slaves.

II

In a generic sense, *The Confessions of Nat Turner* is problematic because it is only ostensibly a legal transcript of sworn testimony. It would more accurately be described as Gray's transcription of Turner's testimony. The recitation of the trial record that Gray reports, for instance, differs in several important areas from the official trial record.[9] And though it combines elements of the religious conversion narrative, it is more closely related to criminal narratives like the *Dying Confession of Pomp, A Negro Man* (1795) or *The Life, and dying speech of Arthur; a Negro man; who was executed at Worcester; October 20th 1768. For a rape committed on the body of one Deborah Metca* (1768), which were part of a popular eighteenth-century subgenre of black narrative writing. But Turner's is not the story of drunken, licentious behavior that both titillates the reader and provides closure through the apprehension of the narrator and the subsequent confession of his misdoings. After finally being captured several months after his revolt (see Illustration 2.1), Nat Turner was encouraged by Thomas R. Gray, a white southern lawyer and slaveholder, to give an account of the reasons behind his activities. Gray served as legal council for some of the other captured slaves, though he did not serve as Turner's legal counsel.[10]

Strictly speaking, Turner's narrative, entitled a "confession" by Gray, was dictated, written, edited, and commented upon (in an intro-

Illustration 2.1. The Discovery of Nat Turner.
The Norfolk Herald, November 4, 1831.

duction, conclusion, and at several places throughout the narrative)
by Gray himself. In this respect, the narrative literally reflects the kind
of mediated environment and anxiety of textual survival through
which black voices before the Civil War were heard. As in other slave
narratives, Gray's editorial voice precedes the voice of the actual narrator, places the narrative in a context for the reader, and, true to the
form of the slave narrative, insists that this narrative is a faithful representation of the narrator's words. What Gray additionally manages to
do is to create for himself a sympathetic, self-authorizing persona that
places Turner beyond the boundaries of white comprehension. For
Gray, the basis of Turner's actions are "entirely local" (*CNT* 42) and
have nothing to do with the repressive institution of slave control
from which they arise.[11]

The question-and-answer format of the narrative allows the reader directly to hear the collision of "voices." The very way in which Turner's presentation of himself is framed within the title of the work indicates the conflict of worldviews.[12] Almost regardless of where the reader is able to locate the precise boundary between Turner's and Gray's respective "voices," what becomes clear is that the convergence of their "voices" in the *Confessions* creates a text very different from the text intended by either Turner or Gray. Furthermore, since the publication of the *Confessions* in 1831, the fruit of their literary and historical partnership has encouraged readers to engage various modes of explication to arrive at some sense of its meaning and significance. All of these approaches require an awareness of the ways in which the imbalance of power, both rhetorical and actual, of slavery itself contributed both to its production and its continued reception. But the imbalance of power, defined by slavery and inscribed in the composition of the text itself, is addressed by Turner in the actuality of his rebellion. In seeking to authorize himself and his actions, he redirects the focus away from merely a localized presentation of origins. Instead, he engages biblical precedent as a way of simultaneously accounting for his actions and for the textual transformation he has made from being the object of Gray's anxious narrative scrutiny to being his own narrative subject.

Turner's initial appearance in his own narrative comes after a series of prefatory elements including a certified statement from the clerk of the District Court for the District of Columbia attesting to the fact that what follows was "fully and voluntarily made to Thomas R. Gray" by Turner and that it is "an authentic account of the whole insurrection"; Thomas R. Gray's introduction; a certified statement from the members of the court convened in Jerusalem, Virginia, for Turner's trial further attesting to the authenticity of Turner's "confessions"; and a certified statement from the clerk of the County Court of Southampton, Virginia, attesting to the fact that those who have signed the statement immediately preceding were "acting Justices of the Peace" . . . "and were members of the Court which convened at Jerusalem" for the trial of Nat Turner. Yet with all of these authorizing elements, Turner's very first words refute Gray's interpretation of his actions: "Sir,—You have asked me to give a history of the motives which induced me to undertake the late insurrection, *as you call it*" (*CNT* 44, emphasis added). In his prefatory material, Gray depicts Turner as a religious fanatic whose band, "actuated by such hellish purposes"

(*CNT* 41) diabolically misread the Bible for their own fiendish purposes. In so doing, Gray's counterdialogue attempts to undercut Turner's discussion of his reasons for doing what he did and offers (possibly inadvertently on Gray's part) as much insight into the thoughts and anxieties of Thomas R. Gray as it does into the thoughts and motives of Nat Turner. It was obvious, for instance, that Gray wanted rhetorically to encapsulate Turner's beliefs and motivations within an enclosure of dementia.[13] Turner's portion of the narrative does nothing to refute this reading and, coupled with his continued references to the religious visions that encourage him to fulfill his apocalyptic role, gives Gray the opportunity to use Turner's own presentation of his unique status against him.

Thus, for Gray, the Christ-like role that Turner seeks to assume can easily be countered by offering an opposing Satanic reading. If nothing else, what becomes clear is that in offering this kind of oppositional framework for reading the text, neither "voice" can fully exist as a freestanding, authorized "voice" on its own. Each "voice" needs the limiting and defining qualities of the other for its own existence and significance. Gray furthermore needed the hysteria created by Turner's insurrection in order to sell the booklet itself. The compressed timeframe of composition (Gray interviewed Turner on November 1–3, 1831, he acquired a copyright on November 10, Turner was hanged on November 11, and the booklet was published in Baltimore less than two weeks later) closely coincides with the fact that Gray' financial fortunes were quickly diminishing from the relative prosperity he enjoyed in 1829, when he had twenty-one slaves and eight hundred acres of land, to the single horse he reported as property just three years later.[14]

Turner's presentation of his own life is thoroughly typological. According to Turner, even as a child he had a naturally religious inclination and one day in the fields had a religious experience: "As I was praying one day at my plough, the spirit spoke to me, saying 'Seek ye the kingdom of Heaven and all things shall be added unto you' " (*CNT* 46).[15] After this experience, Turner's narrative begins to sound like the prophetic revelation presented to John on the isle of Patmos at the conclusion of the New Testament. Turner says that on one occasion "I looked and saw the forms of men in different attitudes—and there were lights in the sky to which the children of darkness gave other names than what they really were—for they were the lights of the Savior's hands, stretched forth from east to west, even as they were extended on the cross on Calvary for the redemption of sinners" (*CNT* 47). It is near this time that Turner's messianic impulses became clear: "I heard a loud noise in the heavens, and the Spirit instantly appeared to me and said the Serpent was loosened, and Christ had laid down the yoke he had borne for the sins of men, and that I should take it on and fight against the Serpent, for the time was fast approaching when the first should be the last and the last should be first.[16] *Ques.* Do you not find yourself mistaken now? *Ans.* Was not Christ crucified" (*CNT* 47–48).

For Gray and the narrative's reading audience, this was undoubtedly blasphemous. But given the shape of Turner's portion of the narrative, the circle was now complete. Turner has presented himself as a Christ-like figure whose responsibility it was to fight against evil and empower those without power. Just as the Old Testament story of Jonah, whose descent into the stomach of a whale and subsequent "reincarnation" after three days, foreshadows Christ's death, burial, and rebirth after three days, so too is Gray's obvious disapproval indicative of Turner's sacrificial qualities. Like Christ before him, Turner was to be executed by a populace that neither believed nor understood his divinity. Turner did not merely see himself as a preacher. He saw himself as a prophet in direct lineage to Christ. The implications are that Turner spiritually stands at the place where blacks would ascend from their lowly status as slaves and whites would finally be punished for their actions. Turner revised the New Testament in the same way Christ revised the Old.[17]

The intersection of religion and Turner's revolt is most clear in his inversion of the scriptural passage from Luke 12: 47 that slaveholders often used to justify their actions: "For he who knoweth his Master's will, and doeth it not, shall be beaten with many stripes, and thus have I chastened you" (*CNT* 46). For Turner, the will of the master did not refer to an earthly master but instead to a heavenly master who expected Turner to fulfill his role as a prophet destined to initiate Judgment Day: "For as the blood of Christ had been shed on this earth, and had ascended to heaven for the salvation of sinners, and was now returning to earth again in the form of dew—and as the leaves on the trees bore the impression of the figures I had seen in the heavens, it was plain to me that the Saviour was about to lay down the yoke he had borne for the sins of men, and the great day of judgment was at hand" (*CNT* 47). As Turner's appropriation suggests, he was able fully to co-opt and invert the language of religion. It became his instrument of change rather than his master's tool of submission. It is not always clear, though, where the language of religion ends and the language of revolution begins. As Turner's example suggests, biblical language warning of the apocalypse could, without a great deal of modification, easily be combined with language expressing a fundamental desire for freedom. This, after all, was one of the basic lessons with which black preachers and their congregations most closely identified in Old Testament stories about the Israelites and their eventual deliverance from Egyptian enslavement. Similarly, many preachers saw themselves as latter-day prophets engaged in a biblical struggle of faith in the face of extreme hardship. In a rhetorical sense, Turner blurred the boundaries between master and slave by using the language to which he was given access and actively interpreting it in a way that more fully represented his sense of his own experience and identity.

As William L. Andrews points out, the conclusion of the narrative emphasizes some of the tensions embodied in it by suggesting that even the rubric of religious fanatic was too limiting for explaining Turner. Turner's ultimate unknowably (and, by extension, the possibility that all blacks existed behind a mask that ultimately obscured true motives and intentions) was what was most disturbing to Gray.[18] For instance, in seeking to try to explain the reasons for Turner's actions and in an attempt to calm southern fears of an organized plot by slaves to overthrow the southern way of life, Gray concludes by saying that "He is a complete fanatic, or plays his part most admirably." But where Andrews sees this as a suggestion that even the category of religious fanatic was ultimately unable fully to define Turner for Gray, it conversely seems more accurate to say that this category is the only category adequate for Gray to absorb Turner's attempts to define and create himself in a larger context of meaning. The narrative's frame as well as Gray's repeated intrusions into and attempts to subvert and reinterpret Turner's text do not necessarily undo or call that into question as much as they emphasize the tensions inherent in Gray's problematic relationship to the text.

III

The structure of Turner's *Confessions* suggests a remarkable sense of fragmentation and plurality of discourse. Gray's parts of the narrative actively seek to restrict Turner's contributions to his own story and try to separate Turner's experiences from the history and experiences to which they refer. Those experiences are turned into a series of untethered images that appear to have no relation to prior experiences. Though Turner's own words refute Gray's attempts to the contrary, the rhetorical environment in which Gray places Turner's story tries to turn that narrative into a series of nonlinear, random events that distance those incidents from the source of those origins. As with slave narratives that are sponsored by sympathetic endorsers, Turner's experiences became the commodity of the culture in which they were produced. The success of the narrative of these particular experiences, at least as they are framed within this commodified region, seem for Gray to be a function of his ability to fragment and isolate Turner's experiences and reactions from the organic cultural context in which they appear. Thus, Gray is free to insist in his brief preface to the narrative that "If Nat's statements can be relied on, the insurrection in this county was entirely local, and his designs confided but to a few, and these in his immediate vicinity" (*CNT* 42). Gray's comments here point toward a more problematic understanding of the situation than an initial reading implies. His words foreshadow Du Bois's thoughts on black double-consciousness by more than half a century and point toward the kinds of masking devices routinely employed by slaves.

As Eric Sundquist notes, the implied meaning encoded in Turner's revolt is that behind the mask of docility and acceptance (what Stanley Elkins's revisionist history of slavery refers to as the "sambo" mentality) lay the possibility of violent reprisal.[19] The most radical views of contemporaneous liberation theology, as represented by David Walker's *Appeal* and Robert Alexander Young's pamphlet *The Ethiopian Manifesto issued in Defense of the Black Man's Rights, in the Scale of Universal Freedom* indicate that violent reprisal is not merely a possibility. Violent reprisal is the logical outgrowth of active religious faith. The question of how the text of that logical outgrowth, the *Confessions*, and its fragmented mode of composition and discourse (within Turner's area of the narrative), is able simultaneously to engage and transcend its theological origins is evident in the way in which Turner liberally appropriates his theological foundation from throughout the Bible. He is a new kind of Christ whose "scripture" is a pastiche of theological thought recombined into a new theology. Slave rebellion is equated with the apocalypse and Nat Turner himself is able to justify his thought by referring to, among others, Jeremiah, Ezekiel, Joel, Matthew, Luke, the Acts, and Revelation. In Jeremiah's prophecies of

impending judgments, God warns that Jerusalem is the place of iniq-
uity and says "Prepare ye war against her [Jerusalem]; . . . Arise, and
let us go by night, and let us destroy her palaces. For thus hath the
Lord of hosts said, Hew ye down trees, and cast a mount against Jerusalem: this is the city to be visited; she is wholly oppression in the
midst of her" (Jeremiah 6: 4–6). Ironically, Jerusalem was the seat of
Southampton County, Virginia, which Turner's reading of the Bible
would not have overlooked.

Turner's narrative suggests that he was aware of holding a special
place in society and, if we are to believe what he says, he interprets all
of his thoughts and activities up to the point of the uprising as preparation for that moment. One of Turner's earliest recollections reveals
him to both himself and his community as a prophet. He writes,

> It is here necessary to relate this circumstance—trifling as it may seem,
> it was the commencement of that belief which has grown with time, and
> even now, sir, in this dungeon, helpless and forsaken as I am, I cannot
> divest myself of. Being at play with other children, when three or four
> years old, I was telling them something, which my mother overhearing,
> said it had happened before I was born—I stuck to my story, however,
> and related somethings which went, in her opinion, to confirm it—oth-
> ers being called on were greatly astonished, knowing that these things
> had happened, and caused them to say in my hearing, I surely would be
> a prophet, as the Lord had shewn me things that had happened before
> my birth (*CNT* 44).

Having connected himself to those things that preceded his birth,
Turner had a vision that connects him to everything that will come
after: "And about this time I had a vision—and I saw white spirits and
black spirits engaged in battle, and the sun was darkened—the thun-
der rolled in the Heavens, and blood flowed in streams—and I heard
a voice saying, 'Such is your luck, such you are called to see, and let it
come rough or smooth, you must surely bare it' " (*CNT* 46). Turner's
vision seems to reflect the prophet Joel's visions of God's judgments
against the enemies of Israel: "And it shall come to pass afterward,
that I will pour out my spirit upon all flesh; and your sons and your
daughters shall prophesy, your old men shall dream dreams, your
young men shall see visions. . . . And I will shew wonders in the heavens and in the earth, blood, and fire, and pillars of smoke" (Joel 2:
28, 30). And according to his testimony, in this instance as much

religious as it is legal, Turner becomes the young visionary toward whom Joel's apocalyptic prophecy looks: "And I . . . discovered drops of blood on the corn as though it were dew from heaven—and I communicated it to many, both white and black, in the neighborhood—and I then found on the leaves in the woods hieroglyphic characters, and numbers, with the forms of men in different attitudes, portrayed in blood, and representing the figures I had seen before in the heavens" (*CNT* 47). If the biblical precedent upon which Turner has thus far grounded his narrative has looked toward the Old Testament, with an emphasis on apocalyptic prophecy and the return of the messiah, Turner's recitation subsequently turns its attention to establishing him as the embodiment of that prophecy.

Turner, at the behest of what he calls the Spirit, prepares to take up Christ's yoke and initiate the apocalyptic struggle that will make the first last and the last first. In this sense, the last will be the slave now empowered by a leader who hears the Word of God and who is willing and able to act according to his understanding of God's will. At this point in the narrative, Gray has interrupted and denied Turner's account three times in ways that parallel Peter's thrice denial of Christ. Gray initially interrupts Turner to question him about what he means by "the Spirit" (*CNT* 46) and implicitly calls into question the "voice" of the deity that animates Turner. During the second interruption, Gray asks if, having semiotically deciphered the signs and symbols of this deity, Turner does not find himself somehow mistaken in his interpretation and subsequent actions. Turner's response ("Was not Christ crucified" [*CNT* 48]) indicates the depth of his association with Christ-like sacrifice. In the context of this Christ-like association, Gray's final question concerns the reasons why Turner was slow to join his co-conspirators for the Last Supper, which initiates their uprising. But as he lets Gray know ("The same reason that had caused me not to mix with them for years before" [*CNT* 48]), Turner was merely fulfilling the role he had assumed in the earliest years of his life. Turner's recitation of his actions and the actions of his group initially seems in stark contrast to the loving, forgiving figure of Christ who appears in the New Testament to revise the teachings of the Old Testament. This section may be seen as the most disturbing passage for Gray's intended audience. Turner himself says that he "had been living with Mr. Joseph Travis, who was to me a kind master, and placed the greatest confidence in me; in fact, I had no cause to complain of his treatment to me" (*CNT* 48). Yet his narrative goes on to detail the way Turner and his group entered the house of this "kind" master and quickly murdered the family as they lay in their beds. If one is to read this kindness correctly, Turner's apocalyptic war has virtually nothing to do with this particular master, the larger institution of slavery, or even his stated objective of reaching Jerusalem. His is a war intended to fulfill his interpretation of biblical prophecy.

This is a primary aspect of the kinds of masking and doubleness that characterize the text. To all concerned, with the obvious exception of the conspirators themselves, Turner and his group were largely happy and contented slaves who knew, and were known by, their community. In his preface to the narrative, Gray writes that "It will thus appear, that whilst every thing upon the surface of society wore a calm and peaceful aspect; whilst not one note of preparation was heard to warn the devoted inhabitants of woe and death, a gloomy fanatic was revolving in the recesses of his own dark, bewildered, and overwrought mind, schemes of indiscriminate massacre to the whites" (*CNT* 41). It was this appearance of calm that was undoubtedly so concerning to southern slaveholding whites. In the moments preceding the rebellion, slaves were virtually invisible to slaveholding whites. But the rebellion itself emphasizes the dangers associated with that assumption. If a slave like Nat Turner could organize and carry out a plan that resulted in the deaths of approximately fifty-five white people, then possibly their own slaves and slaves throughout the South were plotting similar reprisals. Turner serves as the archetypal basis of the unnamed narrator in Ralph Ellison's *Invisible Man*, who realizes the paradox of his invisibility and overcomes that invisibility and lack of identity by producing a narrative that orders and makes sense of his experience.[20]

Turner's reaction to his invisibility is as much physical as it is rhetorical. His is an invisibility (metaphorically depicted by his decision to strike his victims at night, under the cover of darkness) made visible (represented by the trail of dead bodies) that fully reflects Ezekiel's Old Testament vision of Jerusalem when God instructs him to

> Go through the midst of the city, through the midst of Jerusalem, and set a mark upon the foreheads of the men that sigh and that cry for all the abominations that be done in the midst thereof. And to the others he said in mine hearing, Go ye after him through the city, and smite: let

not your eye spare, neither have ye pity: Slay utterly old and young, both maids, and little children, and women: but come not near any man upon whom is the mark; and begin at my sanctuary. Then they began at the ancient men which were before the house" (Ezekiel 9: 4–6).

Having initiated his revolt in accordance with a combination of prophecy appearing in Ezekiel, Joel, and the Acts, Turner begins his movement toward Jerusalem. His group is captured and he himself is eventually captured several months later. At this point near the conclusion of the narrative, Turner's prophetic voice is overtaken by Gray's reassertion of his own presence. Gray is concerned about a concurrent slave rebellion that occurred in North Carolina and the possibility of some kind of collusion in the formulation of their plans. Since Gray has already enshrouded Turner's testimony within the context of religious fanaticism, Turner's response to Gray's stance ("I see sir, you doubt my word; but can you not think the same ideas, and strange appearances about this time in the heaven's might prompt others, as well as myself, to this undertaking" [*CNT* 54]) is both understandable and expected. The final coda to the narrative is entirely Gray's voice, which simultaneously seeks to assuage southern fears of a large-scale slave uprising and to corroborate the factual elements of Turner's account. Gray writes that "[O]n the evening of the third day that I had been with him, I began a cross examination, and found his statement corroborated by every circumstance coming within my own knowledge or the confessions of others whom had been either killed or executed, and whom he had not seen nor had any knowledge since 22d of August last, he expressed himself fully satisfied as to the impracticability of his attempt" (*CNT* 54).

At some level, Gray does seem convinced that Turner's strength extends beyond the physical, when Gray notes that "The calm, deliberate composure with which he spoke of his late deeds and intentions, the expression of his fiend-like face when excited by enthusiasm, still bearing the stains of the blood of helpless innocence about him; clothed with rags and covered with chains; yet daring to raise his manacled hands to heaven, with a spirit soaring above the attributes of man; I looked on him and my blood curdled in my veins" (*CNT* 54–55). Turner's spirit, coupled with a diabolical visage and uncommon intelligence, almost seems to surpass Gray's assessment of Turner as a crazed religious fanatic. Typically, the guarantor of the slave's story sought to place that text in a larger context of political and social meaning. This, with his insistence on the fact that Turner's is an isolated event and unrelated to more generalized slave unrest in the South, is exactly what Gray is trying to do. It seems, though, that since Turner's story has drawn so heavily on theological precedent, Gray needs to find some way to restore religious order along with social order. This may account for Gray's focus in the final paragraph of the narrative on those who escaped death at the hands of Turner's group. The escape of a little girl who hid in a chimney and says that "The Lord helped her" (*CNT* 55) offers an antiphonal voice to Turner's counterclaims of divine assistance. She, in effect, has the last word. Read against the final sentence of the narrative, in which Gray says that "But fortunate for society, the hand of retributive justice has overtaken them; and not one that was known to be concerned has escaped" (*CNT* 56), that justice is as much divine as it is legal. Turner's social fanaticism, bolstered by religious fanaticism, is ultimately overpowered and defeated by the social and theological boundaries it sought to redefine.

The court documents appended at the conclusion of the narrative, along with a list of white people who were killed and black people who were brought before the court, indicates that Nat's "confession" was read before the court before he was asked if he had any final words to say on his own behalf. With his response that "I have not. I have made a full confession to Mr. Gray, and I have nothing more to say" (*CNT* 56), Turner looks toward Melville's use of silence in the character of Babo who, in "Benito Cereno," also declined the opportunity to speak on his own behalf after an unsuccessful slave revolt.[21] Turner's apparent acceptance of Gray's formulation of his narrative may be a reflection of his awareness that the legal proceedings swirling around him were not intended to reflect his own standards of justice and bore no relationship to his own sense of himself.

IV

William L. Andrews points out that the inability of Gray's depiction of Turner as a religious fanatic fully to explain Turner's actions points toward the existence of another mode of thinking fully at odds with accepted white conceptions of reality.[22] Yet what also needs to be taken into account in Gray's assessment of Turner's narrative is that not only another mode of thinking but reason itself is suspect as a component in Turner's motives. By diverting attention to the possibility that when excited by religious enthusiasm Turner could react with cold-hearted violence, Gray makes the implicit point that Turner's violent reaction to slavery is more troubling than the condition of slavery itself. Structurally, the narrative connects Turner's personal history with his rebellion; thus, before Turner can adequately "give a history of the motives" (*CNT* 44) that contributed to his decision to organize his rebellion, he must first give his personal history and the conditions of that personal history: "To do so I must go back to the days of my infancy, and even before I was born. I was thirty-one years of age the 2d of October last, and born the property of Benj. Turner, of this county" (*CNT* 44). Aside from the conditions of Turner's history, that is, the condition of slavery, there is no indication that any of the circumstances particular to that story should have led to the killing of approximately fifty-five white people. Turner depicts his master as relatively kind and as someone who even realizes Turner's intelligence and piousness. While Turner, as William L. Andrews indicates, redirects Gray's question about the origin of the motives for the insurrection into an exposition of his own origins, it is clear that Gray organizes and interprets Turner's actions almost completely in relation to his reading of Turner's religious zealotry.

Since much of what we as readers know about Nat Turner comes from the *Confessions* itself (supplemented by trial documents and contemporaneous newspaper accounts), an understanding of Gray's attitude toward his subject is crucial to a fuller awareness of the text as a whole. Most important is the fact that in failing to see that Turner's actions are largely a function of his status as a slave, Gray implicitly argues that southern social conditions were natural and that Turner, in seeking to undo those social conditions, ultimately violated the essentialist view white southerners had of blacks as chattel. The second part of Turner's confession, in which he describes the killing that takes place during the insurrection itself, serves as the climactic moment of the narrative. His escape and subsequent capture are a mere coda. The legal transcription at the conclusion of the document is not especially illuminating as a source of greater explanation because Turner maintains his silence. While Turner's plea of not guilty would seem inappropriate to Gray's intended audience in light of those "innocent" people who were killed during the insurrection, the structure of the narrative seems to connect that plea of innocence to the earliest parts of the narrative in which Turner focuses on his condition as a slave rather than to his actions on behalf of that innocence. His testimony, as contained in his "confession," indicates that Turner sees his divinely inspired actions in relation to his status as a prophet and a slave and not in relation to those approximately fifty-five white people who died as a result of that status.

As much as Gray attempted to ahistoricize Turner and treat him as some kind of abberration, Gray's underlying assumptions about Turner and the import of his actions place Turner within the accepted codes of conduct and stereotyped roles involving slaves. Gray refers in his "Notice to the Pubic" to "the community" within which Turner's actions took place, as well as to "our widely extended empire" (*CNT* 40). There is, in other words, a clearly defined social arrangement that Turner, who seems to have had kind owners (relatively speaking), an education, and humane living conditions, violates in his unwillingness to accept his socially appointed role as contented slave. Furthermore, the way in which Turner is referred to throughout Gray's text suggests a strategy that seeks to disconnect Turner from ancestral lineage by consistently referring to him simply as "Nat." Even the court documents immediately preceding the confession refer to Turner as "Nat, alias Nat Turner, a negro slave" (*CNT* 42). Yet Turner does have a paternal relationship indicated both by his father's appearance early in the "confession" and by his master's paternalistic presence throughout.

Gray's becomes a parodic version of the "voices" that frame the traditional slave narrative form. Briefly, Gray's "voice" becomes as conflicted as the divided structure of the narrative itself. He says that Turner possesses what he calls an "uncommon share of intelligence," and that Turner's decision to surrender showed the strength of his character rather than any kind of cowardice. But having defended Turner's intelligence and character, he goes on to address the submerged text of what Turner's uprising and narrative mean for the South: The mask of inscrutability and acceptance behind which lurks the possibility of bloody confrontation. For Gray, Turner "is a complete fanatic, or plays his part most admirably" (*CNT* 54). An article published in 1861 by the abolitionist Thomas Wentworth Higginson notes the ways in which Turner was subsequently absorbed by the tradition of the African-American trickster figure.[23] This sounds like a remarkably apocryphal reading of Turner. What is clear, though, is that Higginson and those closest to Turner, including Gray himself, see the realities of the mask and the possibilities of what lurks behind the mask. Seen in relation to his actions, the narrative creates for the reader a splicing together of thought and experience into a whole that struggles against extinction by Thomas R. Gray's presence, as well as by extinction from southern reaction to the narrative. But Turner's "confession" also finds its meaning in the direct conflict of "voices" that his story incorporates.

The acquisition of "voice" may be seen as an ultimate achievement of the former slave.[24] But that acquisition of "voice" reflects for Turner the intensely divided nature of experience he must combine. Turner's is the story of his attempt to combine the sacred with the secular, the enslaved with the free, and the individual, self-isolated prophet with the social needs that prophetic stance required itself to fulfill. Turner struggles to find a "voice," a way of expressing his sense of himself, and this accounts for both his realization that he must attempt to carry out his plan and possibly for his decision to offer his own account of his activities to Gray. If we are to read the slave experience, as many cultural critics do, as an attempt on the part of slaves to find their "voices," then it necessary to insist that there are times when it is simply better not to speak, which is exactly what Turner chooses to do at the conclusion of his "confession." The doubleness of Turner's narrative, in short, reflects the kind of doubleness that defined his life as a prophet detained on a southern plantation until given the sign by the Spirit to begin his sacred responsibilities.

3

"Behold a Man Transformed":
Sacred Language and the Secular Self
in Frederick Douglass's *Narrative*

While [the African American] lives and moves in the midst
of a white civilisation, everything that he touches is re-
interpreted for his own use.
—Zora Neale Hurston, "Characteristics
of Negro Expression"

THE PIVOTAL issue of religion in discussions of Frederick Douglass's *Narrative* has long been a starting point for literary critics interested in discovering how Douglass achieves the rhetorical meaning and effect he does. In one of the more important essays on the subject, Robert O'Meally argues for a reading of the *Narrative* that sees it not only as being influenced by sermons and the sermonic tradition of the African-American preacher, but also as itself being a black sermon that is "a text meant to be preached."[1] And this, in so many ways, is precisely the case. The *Narrative* is as much a text calling for readers to hear the message of the abolitionist movement as it is a recitation of the experiences of Frederick Douglass, an American slave (see Illustration 3.1). The Bible, as Douglass was undoubtedly well aware, was the single most important authorizing text in mid-nineteenth-century American culture. It was the document that was used both to justify the slave system and to call for its abolition.

My interest here is to examine the ways in which Douglass saw religious language and the fervor inscribed in that language, if not the religion itself, as an empowering rhetorical tool. My intention is to view the *Narrative* linguistically rather than strictly in terms of Douglass's particular thoughts on Christianity or even the ways in which Douglass himself may have been used by Protestant rhetoric. This is

Illustration 3.1. Frederick Douglass in his late twenties.
Unidentified artist, circa 1844. National Portrait Gallery,
Smithsonian Institution, Washington, D.C.

not an attempt to offer a critique of Douglass's critique of American Christianity and certainly not an attempt to examine Douglass's religiosity, especially since he does not offer a specific scene of religious conversion in the *Narrative*. Instead of undergoing a traditional religious conversion, Douglass's presentation of his conversion from a slave to a man occurs in the tenth chapter, in which he relies neither on his friend Sandy Jenkins's root nor on the benevolence of the Christian God. Instead, Douglass depends on his own actions physically to overcome Edward Covey and eventually engineer his escape. Rather than focus on some manifestation of Douglass's moral code in relation to Christianity, I wish to concern myself with the ways Douglass was able not only to use religion and the sermonic tradition to engage the religious rhetoric with which his readers would have been so familiar, but also able to transform that language into a text of his own that authorized his position in the culture and created an individual identity for himself firmly based on the entitling power of biblical precedent.

I

As Ralph Ellison's unnamed narrator asserts about his own narrative in *Invisible Man*, Douglass's end, in which he was similarly made visible by a rhetorical realization and mastering of his own invisibility, was also in his beginning. And like Douglass, that beginning signaled a paradoxical ending. Ellison's narrator faces a series of humiliating experiences throughout the novel in which what he is allowed to say must agree with the agendas of those who provide him the platform to speak. Douglass's *Narrative* begins with Garrison's preface explaining his recollection of first hearing Douglass speak at the Nantucket antislave convention and concludes with Douglass's own reactions to speaking at that convention. The narrative is encircled by William Lloyd Garrison's "voice," which attempts to define the meaning of Douglass's message. But in a larger sense, it is the context of the Nantucket antislave convention that circumscribes the potential contained in the *Narrative*.

In addition to the other nineteenth-century extraliterary elements that shaped fugitive slave stories, there was an oral component that was as much a function of the African oral tradition as it was of New England abolitionist requirements. Abolitionist gatherings regularly included former slaves, like Douglass, who were asked to render the stories of their lives. It is probable that one of the ways Douglass and subsequent slave narrators sharpened the focus of the scenes they chose to include in their narratives was to render them first as oral presentations and gauge the effectiveness of various combinations of experiences. If white abolitionists can be seen as controlling the literary form of expression for ex-slaves (at least in terms of the fugitive slave narrative), then narrative writers themselves may be seen as controlling and mediating the black experience for a white readership.

Clearly though, one of the elements that served to encourage some black writers to choose this form was the fact that the rise of Garrisonian abolitionism provided ex-slaves with a platform, literally and figuratively, upon which blacks could express themselves in terms of their status as former slaves. Before the Garrisonian years, runaway slaves worked to disguise that fact. But Garrison (see Illustration 3.2) was able to see in the social configuration of New England the opportunity to designate and define the direction and tone of the antislavery movement there. In Garrison's mind, New England already had the necessary antislavery sentiments. It simply lacked organizations and a focal center, which he hoped to provide. In the first issue of *The Liberator*, Garrison noted this point:

> During my recent tour for the purpose of exciting the minds of people by a series of discourses on the subject of slavery, every place that I visited gave fresh evidence of the fact, that a greater revolution in public sentiment was to be effected in the free states—and particularly New England—than at the South. I found contempt more bitter, opposition more active, detraction more relentless, prejudice more stubborn, and apathy more frozen than among slave owners themselves. Of course there were individual expectations to the contrary.[2]

One of the strengths of Garrison's attempts to frame antislavery sentiment in New England was that he was able to define the issue in clear, oppositional tones. He provided few areas of nuance for the public to sort through and possibly distract themselves from what he saw as the issues at hand.

This approach to defining the slave issue for New Englanders was very similar to the ways slave narratives distilled the lives and experiences of their narrators into highly concentrated renderings. The notion of "rendering" is especially important here because it speaks the performative aspects of the recounting of experience. Performance

Illustration 3.2. William Lloyd Garrison. Unidentified artist, circa 1855. National Portrait Gallery, Smithsonian Institution, Washington, D.C.

makes itself apparent in the oral aspects of the recitation in front of an audience at antislavery rallies as well as in the literary performance that grows, directly in many instances, out of this oral exhibition.

Southerners came to realize by the 1830s, if not long before, that the slave system was so deeply entrenched in the foundations of the southern economic structure that its abolition would bring an end to southern financial stability.[3] It is out of this context that fugitive slaves began to trickle North. They knew from the growing animosity between the North and the South that the North offered them at least the possibility of a haven. And as they began to arrive, they were co-opted by antislave organizations in the North to tell their story to eager listeners interested in the adventure of violence, deception, and escape that characterized the rhetorical lives of the narrators. The tremendous amount of drama contained in most narratives alone assured fugitive slave writers of a certain level of readership.

In order to sustain the appropriate level of drama, slave narrators increasingly began to focus the narratives on the escape sequences of their stories rather than using their narratives strictly to argue for an ideology of emancipation. This is, no doubt, partially an effect of the entrenchment of southern thought regarding slavery, partially a function of what abolitionists wanted slaves to talk about in oral narratives presented at antislavery rallies, and what they wanted former slaves to write about in their narratives (see Illustration 3.3). Slaves were encouraged to tell their stories in the North, but their access to audiences was closely overseen by their antislavery colleagues.

In the concluding portion of the *Narrative*, Douglass writes that "while attending an anti-slavery convention at Nantucket, on the 11th of August, 1841," he "felt strongly moved to speak."[4] This was not the first time Douglass had been moved to speak; he had previously spoken at a "colored people's meeting in New Bedford" (*N* 96). But the thing that apparently made this public presentation of his story significant is that he overcame his fear of speaking to white people and spoke at a white convention: "The truth was, I felt myself a slave, and the idea of speaking to white people weighed me down" (*N* 96).[5] Douglass overcomes his fear of speaking before white audiences and describes his thoughts on the antislavery movement in terms that could easily be used to describe a religious experience. After reading *The Liberator*, Douglass writes that his "soul was set all on fire" (*N* 96). He leaves the Nantucket convention feeling "a degree of freedom" (*N* 96) and looking forward to carrying his message forward to others. The language at the end of the *Narrative*, coupled as it is with a description of the soul-stirring power of the revival-meeting-tinged spirit of the antislavery convention, turns Douglass's realization of freedom into a public exhibition of renewed fervor.

Anne Kibbey argues that Douglass's public discovery of his "voice" indicates that he has "both discovered and affirmed his freedom fully

Illustration 3.3. Frederick Douglass (seated at the table, right of center) at an outdoor abolitionist rally. Madison County Historical Society, Oneida, New York.

in the linguistic expression of his humanity."[6] Or, as Robert O'Meally suggests, the *Narrative* may be seen as a secular sermon "pitting the dismal hell of slavery against the bright heaven of freedom."[7] And to a large extent these views are very much the case. But Douglass has not simply left slavery behind linguistically or created a secular sermon using freedom and slavery in the same ways a minister would use heaven and hell. Rather, Douglass has managed to use those elements to present a critique of slavery that is rhetorically so firmly rooted in the usual sermonic justifications of slavery that the critique itself becomes a sermonic analysis and self-created representation of his own identity. Because of the encircling frame of William Lloyd Garrison and the Nantucket antislavery convention, Douglass's "voice" in the *Narrative* achieves a consistency of tone and outlook. This suggests a reading of the *Narrative* that places it beyond the framework of the sermon and the spiritual conversion narratives that contribute to the tradition from which fugitive slave narrative writing arose.

In the tradition of slave narrative writing, William Lloyd Garrison's preface to Douglass's *Narrative* serves the dual purposes of introducing Douglass to the reading audience and suggesting to that audience how the *Narrative* should be read. This was a standard feature of the slave narrative genre. But Garrison's preface also serves, either knowingly or unknowingly, to connect Douglass's words to a larger sense of authority and intention. Douglass concludes his *Narrative* by writing "From that time until now I have been engaged in pleading the cause of my brethren—with what success, and with what devotion, I leave those acquainted with my labors to decide" (*N* 96). And this evaluation is exactly what Garrison provides in his preface, which begins with the sentence "In the month of August, 1841, I attended an anti-slavery convention in Nantucket, at which it was my happiness to become acquainted with Frederick Douglass, the writer of the following Narrative" (*N* 4). But Douglass's final words in the *Narrative* and Garrison's opening words in the preface create a paradoxical tension between the timelessness of the *Narrative* itself and its framing criticism, which is firmly rooted in time and historical space.

The *Narrative* ultimately seeks to unite these two apparently unreconcilable positions by suggesting that the act of speaking and writing confers an immediate sense of self-defining power. But more than anything, the oppositional, though complimentary, nature of time and historical space indicates that in order to complete itself, the self-authorizing aspect of the *Narrative* requires more than any particular performance in any distinct context. So when Douglass locates his speech at the Nantucket convention as the context in which he began to feel "a degree of freedom" (*N* 96), it seems only natural that Garrison should say of Douglass that "I shall never forget his first speech at the convention" (*N* 3) because the performance of that speech required Douglass's act of speaking, the context in which the speech could be rendered, and the audience.

Douglass's act of self-fashioning becomes the function of a multilayered context. Before Douglass has an opportunity to assert his own "voice," the *Narrative* opens with Garrison's representation of Douglass's "voice" (though not Douglass's actual words) and with the reaction Douglass's story caused Garrison ("I shall never forget his first speech at the convention—the extraordinary emotion it excited in my own mind" [*N* 3]) and the rest of the audience ("the powerful impression it created upon a crowded auditory, completely taken by surprise—the applause which followed from the beginning to the end of his felicitous remarks" [*N* 3]). "As a public speaker," Garrison writes of Douglass, "he excels in pathos, wit, comparison, imitation, strength of reasoning, and fluency of language" (*N* 5). Garrison would have us believe that these same qualities have been transferred to the *Narrative*.

But what of Garrison's presentation of Douglass's act of speech? As a way of emphasizing the ways in which slavery steals language and the ability to reason, Garrison inserts a story in his preface of an American sailor who becomes enslaved in Africa for three years. During this time, he apparently lost the ability to communicate in English and "could only utter some savage gibberish between Arabic and English, which nobody could understand, and which even he himself found difficulty in pronouncing" (*N* 6). Garrison ostensibly includes this story in order to emphasize slavery's dehumanizing influence, as well as Douglass's exceptional ability to overcome that influence. But it is especially revealing in what it says about Douglass. Unlike the unfortunate sailor, Douglass was able to negotiate the hybrid linguistic space he was required to occupy, which was so reflective of the composite societal position as a "former slave" he occupied between slave and freeman. As Garrison noted earlier, Douglass's ability to imitate is important because he is able to speak and write in a manner that marks him as something other than the "imbruted and stultified" sailor, whose enslavement took from him the ability to communicate.

It seems only fitting, then, that following this story Garrison should turn his attention to alerting the reader that "Mr. Douglass has very properly chosen to write his own *Narrative*, in his own style, and according to the best of his ability, rather than to employ some one else" (*N* 7). The connection between these two areas is not unproblematic, though. Garrison's American sailor story points toward an indictment of the slave system, which "has a natural, an inevitable tendency to brutalize every noble faculty of man" (*N* 6). Even the white sailor was unable to maintain a sense of linguistic self-determination against the savage onslaught of language he encountered. Garrison's preface does not adequately address how Douglass was able to outpace the boundaries of the slave system, especially when we realize that while Douglass had been a slave for most of his life, the sailor described in the story had only been enslaved for three years.[8] The story, however, does address a primary concern of the *Narrative*, which is linguistic acquisition and the importance of the narrator's ability to tell a story and create and maintain an identity.

The stranded sailor becomes metaphorically representative of an inversion of what Ngũgĩ wa Thiong'o sees as the denigration of local language at the expense of the colonizers.[9] The hybrid language in which the sailor speaks parodies the usual pattern in which indigenous language is discarded in favor of the language of the colonizer. Garrison's story emphasizes Ngũgĩ's belief that both the language and the individual employing that language are, at the very least, irreparably changed and, more likely, destroyed by the interaction.[10]

I have suggested earlier that the stories of former slaves were told in collaboration between storyteller and audience. This is clearly the case with the way Douglass presents his acquisition of linguistic freedom at the Nantucket convention as well as the apparent collaboration that is going on between Garrison's preface and the *Narrative* itself. The preface reserves for itself an interpretive function. The structure of the *Narrative* initiates a symbolic pattern in which Douglass is required to transfer the passion embedded in the immediacy of the abolitionist platform speaker's recitation of experience to the printed page. Thus, when Garrison emphasizes that the *Narrative* is entirely Douglass's "own production" and "that it comes short of the reality, rather than overstates a single fact in regard to slavery as it is" (*N* 7), he overstates the level of autonomy that Douglass enjoyed as he formulated his *Narrative*. As the American sailor story suggests, Douglass's success as a storyteller was very much a function of his ability adequately to negotiate the narrow space of linguistic acquisition and communication restrained by the realities of his life as a slave.

Interestingly, in the hyperbole of his introductory remarks, Garrison seems to misread the *Narrative* in several important ways. One of the things Garrison emphasizes is that "nothing is exaggerated, nothing drawn from the imagination" (*N* 7). The passage to which he refers as being especially thrilling is Douglass's famous apostrophe to the Chesapeake, in which Douglass endows the receding ships with all of his sense of longing and desire for freedom. Yet this area, along with Douglass's imagined description of his grandmother's abandonment following the slave auction, is one of the more imaginatively rendered passages in the *Narrative*. The fact is that this allegorized, figurative fiction crept not only into a slave narrative conscientiously certified for its historical accuracy and narratological understatement and restraint but also into an endorsement of the narrative contained in its antiphonal frame story. This serves to indicate the interpolation of Douglass's particular rhetorical construction of experience and response.

One of the recurrent critiques of the fugitive slave narrative genre concerns the way in which narratives all begin to sound alike because of the emphasis on form and content and the de-emphasis of personal characterization. But in the fashion of the African-American oral storytelling (and narrative) tradition, Douglass is able to combine remarkably meticulous passages describing struggle and an intense desire to survive with imaginatively presented areas of fiction that he most likely initially presented orally and subsequently revised and reconfigured as necessary in the *Narrative*. I will develop these points more fully during my discussion of the *Narrative* itself. But in specific relation to Garrison's American sailor story and his erroneous endorsement of Douglass's imaginatively rendered passages in the context of a larger endorsement of the essential unvarnished truth of the *Narrative*, the point I would like to make here is that unlike Garrison's sailor, Douglass was able to find a way to negotiate both the intermixed nature of African-American slave language and the equally crossbred realities of dominant American discourse. Douglass was able to master (with all the various meanings that word contains) the ability required to reinterpret his experiences into a form acceptable to his audience.

The *Narrative* becomes representative of Du Bois's doubleness when it is read as a critical performance in conjunction with the imaginative performance of self-creation and self-authorization. The encircling nature of Garrison's presence in the *Narrative* implies both the encircling, enabling presence of the antislavery movement and the circular, unfinished nature of Douglass's experience.[11]

II

I began this chapter with a discussion of the oral influences encircling the *Narrative*. Douglass, though, undoubtedly absorbed various techniques from the literature he had read. The decision to write in the narrative form was, for him, a conscious decision to write in a particular style for a particular audience.[12] But there was also a distinct desire on the part of black abolitionists to assume some control of ex-slave recitations of the slave experience. The *Freedman's Journal*, an early black newspaper published in New York City, argued for this

point while simultaneously pointing out a certain amount of patroniz-
ing tolerance it had begun to notice among white abolitionists. In the
first issue, from March 16, 1827, the editorial made mention of this
kind of condescension:

> [O]ur friends . . . seem to have fallen into the current of popular feeling
> and are imperceptibly floating in the stream—actually living in the prac-
> tice of prejudice, while they abjure it in theory. . . . Is it not very de-
> sireable that such should know more of our actual condition; and of our
> efforts and feelings, that in forming plans for our amelioration, they may
> do it more understandingly?[13]

These kinds of questions surrounding the paternalistic attitude of
white abolitionists recurred on several occasions and, as with the
Freedman's Journal editorial, often centered on whose "voice" was the
truly authentic "voice" of the slave experience.

The Reverend Henry Highland Garnet (see Illustration 3.4), himself a former slave, advised members of the Negro National convention in 1843 to recommend that slaves adopt a passively resistant
method to achieve their freedom. He suggested that slaves simply re-
fuse to work and demand their freedom. Slaveholders would not agree
to such a proposal and would most likely resort to violence, at which
point the slaves would be morally justified in revolting. This proposal
was voted down by the constituency in favor of more direct, more
assertive methods. Maria Weston Chapman, who frequently acted as
an editor for Garrison's *Liberator*, reacted in a way that Garnet perceived to be contemptuous and derisive. He responded by essentially
telling her that only former slaves can truly know the effects of slavery
and that former slaves like Garnet himself served "to tell you, and
others, what the monster had done and is doing."[14]

Frederick Douglass addressed this issue of slaves speaking for themselves when he wrote in the first issue of the *North Star* on December
3, 1847, that "the man who has suffered the wrong is the man to
demand redress—that the man struck is the man to cry out—and that
he who has endured the cruel pangs of slavery is the man to advocate
liberty." In this same editorial, Douglass goes on to argue that "in the
grand struggle for liberty and equality now waging it is meet, right
and essential that there should arise in our ranks authors and editors,
as well as orators, for it is in the former capacities that the most permanent good can be rendered our cause." For Douglass, African Ameri-

Illustration 3.4. Henry Highland Garnet. James U. Stead, circa 1881.
National Portrait Gallery, Washington, D.C.

cans needed to "be our own representatives and advocates, not exclusively but peculiarly; not distinct from, but in connection with our white friends."[15] To some extent, then, Douglass recognized and even encouraged a certain amount of mediation or, more precisely, collaboration, in order to achieve his goals. The *Narrative* may be seen as being framed by the acceptance of this kind of collaboratist stance. Similarly, the text of the *Narrative* itself also reflects more subtle kinds of collaborations.

Just as Douglass claims to have initially found his social authority within the communal aspects of the abolitionist movement, he found his rhetorical authority in the legitimizing aspects of biblical precedent. In the generic tradition of slave narrative writing, the actual *Narrative* begins by expressing the particulars, minus the date of birth, of Douglass's life: "A want of information concerning my own [date of birth] was a source of unhappiness to me even during childhood. The white children could tell their ages. I could not tell why I ought to be deprived of the same privilege" (*N* 15). As Douglass presents it, the dilemma lay more in his inability to tell his age (or tell why he was deprived of the privilege of doing so) than his inability to know his age. By locating the origins of his *Narrative* within the resolutely indeterminate cyclical space available to slaves for reckoning their dates of birth ("planting-time, harvest-time, cherry-time, spring-time, or fall-time" [*N* 15]), Douglass is able rhetorically to create himself in the gap between knowing and telling. The realities of that split, though, required Douglass to acknowledge the distinction between knowing and telling and thereby emphasize the telling of the story over and above the reality of its origins.

Ironically, if the origins of Douglass's own existence were subverted by his inability to tell his origins, Douglass shows how the slave system obliterated the existence of paternal origins altogether when he writes that "My father was a white man. He was admitted to be such by all I ever heard speak of my parentage. The opinion was also whispered that my master was my father; but of the correctness of this opinion, I know nothing; the means of knowing was withheld from me" (*N* 15). While Douglass cannot fully substantiate the truth of the opinion regarding his father, he can fully incorporate that sense of ambiguity into his presentation of himself in the opening of his *Narrative*. Though the telling of the story transcends the basis of the knowledge, it seems clear in this opening chapter that Douglass is seeking to establish origin and connection within the context of an antithetical language (telling vs. not-knowing) that seems to deny the possibility of achieving that goal.

The very structure of the chapter seems to reinforce the antithetical nature of the language. If the first part of the chapter may be seen as an expression of the indeterminate nature of Douglass's origins, the second part of the chapter may be seen as completing the cycle. In the same way that Douglass is unable fully to define his paternity, he is also unable fully to explain the antithetical relationship between Christianity and the slave. But again, within the apparent space between the reality of the two, Douglass manages to create connection within a context that apparently denies that possibility. The sidelong view Douglass presents of his master's possible paternity is balanced by the sidelong view he presents of his mother: "I never saw my mother, to know her as such, more than four or five times in my life; and each of these times was very short in duration, and at night. . . . I do not recollect ever seeing my mother by the light of day. She was with me in the night. She would lie down with me, and get me to sleep, but long before I waked she was gone" (*N* 16). So, while the abolitionist cause encouraged the use of verifiable facts in the construction of the personal histories of former slaves, Douglass has remarkably few to offer. If Douglass was aware, as his comments concerning the Nantucket antislavery convention seem to indicate, that his story occupied a place that was part of a considerably larger network of gatherings, writings, and political agendas, then he would have understood the importance of acknowledging and using the marginalized space between his precarious life as a slave and the life he could rhetorically create containing deeper structures of connection and coherence.

III

I have emphasized the space Douglass occupied as a way of suggesting, as does Waldo Martin in *The Mind of Frederick Douglass*, that as a person with biracial parentage living as chattel in the midst of the nineteenth-century slave system, Douglass's narratological presentation of himself discloses a great deal about blacks and whites as well as his disposition about his sense of his relationship to African-American culture in particular and American culture in general. There is a deep sense of Du Boisian "doubleness" to the shape of Douglass's life and the way in which Douglass rhetorically presents his life in his writing and gingerly attempts to reconcile his own position within American and African-American cultures. Douglass exemplifies what Du Bois describes in *The Souls of Black Folk* as "two souls, two thoughts, two unreconciled strivings: two warring ideals in one dark body, whose dogged strength alone keeps it from being torn asunder."[16] The opening paragraph of the *Narrative* suggests a Douglass who was remarkably ambivalent about his father, but also intensely interested in his own genealogical origins. This may partially be a function of the constraints of the genre in which he wrote as well as the fact that Douglass's life spanned a time in American culture characterized by an intense self-consciousness about cultural and social identities. Thus, as a former slave narrating the story of his life, Douglass became a representative figure simultaneously suggesting both the fragmentation and interconnection of cultural and political forces that defined his existence. The very existence of the *Narrative* indicates the ultimate act of linguistic acquisition and self-representation within a very limiting and confining cultural matrix.

As Waldo Martin argues, Douglass saw American identity as being the incorporation of some previous national identity into a new one that included but suppressed the old. But his writings subsequent to the *Narrative* indicate a peculiar disjunction regarding racial equality and cultural hierarchy. Douglass believed that each race possessed gifts particular to that race. But these gifts, which he sees as a broad combination of ethical and intellectual qualities, were a function of the environment in which they existed. Because of this, they were therefore alterable. For Douglass, the notion of racial purity was detrimental to cultural development because racial purity was unnatural. Racial and, by extension, cultural miscegenation was the norm.[17]

In a narratological sense, Douglass represents this cultural miscegenation in terms of language and linguistic control. By that, I mean that the *Narrative* clearly functions in the mode of the classic slave narrative and includes standard features like prefatory material from white abolitionist supporters, recitals of beatings and slave life, and descriptions of escape attempts. And as with many slave narratives, it ends with freedom in the North. But there is also a strong linguistic component, characterized by Douglass's emphasis on the importance of literacy, the barriers he overcame to achieve that literacy, and the association he makes between physical liberty and rhetorical freedom.

The Nantucket convention therefore serves as the occasion on which Douglass is first able rhetorically to place the story of his life within a larger cultural context. His "voice," as reflected in the *Narrative*, becomes both an individual "voice" and a cultural product. Since Douglass never fails to ground his rhetorical and literary insights within the larger context of the cultural moment, the *Narrative* resists being seen simply as the story of a detached individual acting in rebellion against his social condition. His is an individual presence that gains meaning from its intersubjective arrangement. But Douglass's grim presentation of his life as a slave and his eventual escape is not nearly as straightforward and uncomplicated as it might seem. As I discussed earlier, Douglass presumably presented orally, at the Nantucket convention and subsequent antislavery rallies, portions of his *Narrative* that he eventually wrote down. Having told his reader of the context in which he found his "voice," it is impossible for the reader not to be aware of the performative aspects of the *Narrative*. But implicit in this understanding is the realization that the speeches and, by extension, the written *Narrative* became shaped by the expectations of the audience and the conventions of the abolitionist sponsors. It ceased to be simply the heartfelt "voice" of African-American slavery and instead became a literary representation of the cultural moment, inscribed with all of the influences and meanings contained in that moment. And Douglass, I think, was well aware of this. We can safely assume that during the oral renderings of his story, Douglass included and expanded scenes to which his audience reacted favorably and dropped or reshaped scenes that the audience seemed less enthusiastic about. Further, given Douglass's awareness of his audience, we can be sure that he sought to give his story meaning and moral weight for that audience by connecting it to the Bible, which was the single most important authenticating document in mid-nineteenth-century American culture.

How exactly does Douglass do this? I have indicated that the preface, central scene, and conclusion of the *Narrative* all point the reader toward Douglass's intense awareness of the importance of literacy and linguistic control. But one of the earliest examples of that control occurs at the conclusion of the first chapter of the *Narrative* when Douglass as a young child witnesses the brutal beating of his Aunt Hester by her master, Captain Anthony. Beating scenes were fairly common features of slave narrative writing and served as a way for the ex-slave narrator to depict the arbitrary and brutal aspects of the system and the effect they had on individuals. In many ways that was the intention of the slave narrative genre itself: To personalize an impersonal system and to show that all who were touched by the system, including slave and master, were ultimately dehumanized by it. At the risk of overanalyzing this brief episode, my objective is to make a case for seeing this scene as illustrating Douglass's way of creating a rhetorical identity that created a new meaning by imposing the experiences of one culture upon another.

The particulars of the scene are that Hester's master, Captain Anthony, had ordered Douglass's Aunt Hester not to go out for the evening. But she did go out and was discovered by Captain Anthony in the company of another slave, Ned Roberts. Anthony took Hester into the kitchen and began to beat her viciously. Douglass tells the reader that "I was so terrified and horror-stricken at the sight, that I hid myself in a closet, and dared not venture out until long after the bloody transaction was over. I expected it would be my turn next. It was all new to me. I had never seen any thing like it before" (*N* 19). But where does the cultural miscegenation that I earlier mentioned occur? Well, remember, Douglass has told his reader that he surreptitiously witnessed the scene while hidden in a closet, terrified that he would be next to receive a similar beating. Douglass here receives instruction about slavery—an instruction probably as important as the instruction he subsequently receives from his mistress in learning to read—that he narratologically imposes upon (or miscegenates, if you will) an Old Testament archetypal scene of biblical instruction: Ham witnessing his father Noah's nakedness and being cursed. In the *Narrative*, Douglass's reenactment of that episode, which he refers to as "the blood-stained, the entrance to the hell of slavery, through which I was about to pass" (*N* 18), is transformed into a scene in which both Douglass and the reader are metaphorically placed in that closet where they together witness the impotent nakedness of the slave system in its violent reprisal against Aunt Hester.[18]

What Douglass does here is to combine an overtly realistic presentation of slavery with an archetypal biblical account of transgression and retribution. Douglass implicitly suggests a connection with Noah, who uses patriarchal authority to control his son in much the same way that southern slave rhetoric sought to control the slave population and maintain social and economic control. But Douglass seems to do a great deal more than simply present the modes of aggression and control used by the slave system. He makes his reader complicit with his own experiences by placing the reader in a voyeuristic position in which he or she is (presumably) as shocked and disgusted by the misdirected authority of a slaveowner seeking to assert his power and authority as is Douglass.[19]

But it is Douglass, at least through the narratological distance of his narrative, who is in control here and asserting his rhetorical power and authority. Immediately preceding the scene in which Douglass and his reader witness Aunt Hester's beating from the kitchen closet, Douglass directly engages the cursing of Ham, which served as the biblical injunction justifying the enslavement of the black race. But Douglass brings even this into the reality of the cultural context. He writes:

> [I]t is nevertheless plain that a very different-looking class of people are springing up at the south, and are now held in slavery, from those origi- nally brought to this country from Africa; and if their increase will do no other good, it will do away with the force of the argument, that God cursed Ham, and therefore American slavery is right. If the lineal descendants of Ham are alone to be scripturally enslaved, it is certain that slavery in the south must soon become unscriptural; for thousands are ushered into the world, annually, who, like myself, owe their exis- tence to white fathers, and those fathers most frequently their own mas- ters (N 17–18).

Several things are going on here that will return this chapter to that oppositional intersection between cultural studies, literature, and racial politics from whence I began. First, Douglass seems to be locat- ing the point of weakness for the slaveholder at what is apparently the slaveholder's greatest strength: The slaveholder's control of language. Douglass sees that control as ultimately lacking the ability to make reality. There is a deep gap, according to Douglass's formulation, be- tween the master's use of language and the reality that it describes. Douglass makes pointed reference to that linguistic weakness by di- rectly connecting it to his own apparent control of language and meaning in his presentation of the Aunt Hester scene. He also ironi- cally criticizes arbitrary distinctions between slave and free by noting the miscegenistic relationship between masters and slaves, as well as the cultural miscegenation inherent in the slave system.[20]

Douglass concludes the first chapter by writing that "I had always lived with my grandmother on the outskirts of the plantation . . ." (N 19) and begins the second chapter with a description of plantation life in general and Colonel Lloyd's Great House Farm in particular. Just as Douglass describes himself as witnessing the beating of his Aunt Hester from outside the "blood-stained gate" of slavery, and thus rendering himself unable fully to understand its meaning, he is paradoxically also blinded to the realities of slave life because of being inside the circle. Douglass's description of slave singing mirrors, to some extent, Garrison's story of the sailor who became so imbruted that he forgot his native language and was only able to express himself in an unrecognizable hybrid language. Douglass's slave community also communicates in what could be regarded as an unrecognizable hybrid language. Or, more precisely, in a hybrid discourse deeply misinterpreted by all but those who were a part of it. And again, as with the origins of Douglass's *Narrative* at the Nantucket convention, there is a strong performative element: "[T]hey would sing, as a chorus, words which to many would seem unmeaning jargon, but which, nevertheless, were full of meaning to themselves" (*N* 23–24). The difference between Garrison's unfortunate sailor and Douglass's position outside the chorus seems to be the importance of a community within which "unmeaning jargon" is transformed into meaningful communication. The incomprehensible babblings of the solitary sailor become transformed into the singing of a chorus of slaves who only themselves understand the true meaning of their songs.

But here Douglass adds a curious comment about his own relationship to the meaning encoded in the sorrow songs: "I did not, when a slave, understand the deep meaning of those rude and apparently incoherent songs. I was myself within the circle; so I neither saw nor heard as those without might see and hear" (*N* 24). Douglass's reason for this apparent shift is unclear. He suggests that meaning is a function of being a part of the community. However, he locates himself within that community ignorant of the true meaning of the songs while claiming that those outside the community had a better comprehension of the meaning than he. But as Douglass also notes, those outside of the slave community often misunderstand the true meaning of the sorrow songs: "I have often been utterly astonished, since I came to the north, to find persons who could speak of the singing, among slaves, as evidence of their contentment and happiness. It is impossible to conceive of a greater mistake" (*N* 24). Douglass's self-established position both within and without the community reflects that of the young boy who watched from the closet as his Aunt Hester was beaten, terrified that he himself would be next to receive a similar punishment.

In the passage in which Aunt Hester is beaten, Douglass occupied a similar position both within and without the circle. There, he witnessed, without experiencing it himself, the physical reality of what it was to be a slave. And most importantly, he was able eventually to construct a narrative that created a context and meaning for that experience. In that particular case, he drew on biblical precedent to reinforce the meaning of his experience. In his description of the sorrow songs, he simultaneously stands within and outside the circle, understanding yet not understanding the true meaning of the singing. The initiation he receives may be read in relation to the initiation he subsequently faces in terms of the ways in which northerners misunderstood black expression. But Douglass's role remains the same. He is able to understand, at some level, the rude and apparently incomprehensible jargon of the songs and to convey some sense of that meaning to a readership that responded to the expression of the message (the singing) without fully comprehending the meaning embedded in that expression. It is unclear why Douglass chose to present himself as simultaneously within the circle of the slave experience and therefore unknowing of the meaning of the songs and outside of the experience and knowledgeable about the meaning of the songs, but it seems plausible that the various, miscegenated nature of Douglass's self-created position (slave/former slave, inside/outside, not understanding/understanding) reflects the miscegenated nature of Douglass's racial background.

This miscegenated self that Douglass presents in his *Narrative*, as well as the divided self that he presents as in-but-not-necessarily-of the experience is an important constructive act in mid-nineteenth-century America, where race played such a crucial role as an important defining feature. By this, I mean to suggest that in a narratological sense, Douglass has created a middle-ground persona who observes, who has been both within and outside the circle, and who performs the service of communicating black experience and interpreting the meaning inscribed in that experience for those of his (presumably) white reading audience who had no firsthand experience with either slavery or the black experience.

The rhetorical space he creates in the *Narrative* is in many ways remarkably similar to the position he occupies as a person of biracial parentage living in the South whose master is his father. Douglass sees the master's acknowledged children and the benefits they enjoy and realizes that because of his black ancestry, which legally decrees "that the children of slave women shall in all cases follow the tradition of the mothers" (*N* 16–17), he can never fully acknowledge that side of himself. But as much as he cannot fully acknowledge his father, so too can he never be fully within the circle of slavery. He becomes a type of tragic mulatto figure. But Douglass was, by the time he sat down to construct the *Narrative*, fully aware of the unique nature of his position in American society. Part of the difficulty is that in constructing the *Narrative*, Douglass had to find a way to reconcile a position that was as much cultural as it was personal and political. The within/without construction of how Douglass describes his understanding of the meaning of the songs suggests some of the difficulty he had in reconciling these positions.

This difficult position is also reflected in Douglass's subsequent writings and civil rights work. He noted, in a speech delivered to a group of Tennessee farmers almost thirty years after the publication of the *Narrative*, that due to the residual effects of slavery, African Americans had acquired bad habits, namely thoughtlessness and improvidence, that had to be mitigated by the acquisition of what he perceived as European-American values of thought and providence.[21] In making a case for other African Americans to adopt European standards, Douglass does what he has implicitly done in his description of his Aunt Hester's beating and what he has explicitly achieved in his description of the sorrow songs, which is to separate himself either physically or ideologically from the realities of the situation he describes. He was physically hidden in a closet during the Aunt Hester passage and, in his description, ideologically distanced through the overlay of the biblical Ham story. In the sorrow songs passage, his distancing is a function of his inability to understand the true meaning of the songs while he was within the circle. Though culturally and politically placed in a position in which he was forced to be either one thing or another, Douglass creates a rhetorical space for himself in which he is both one thing and another.

But in creating this rather complicated rhetorical space for himself, Douglass was working very directly within the context of a current of thought that was extremely influential during the mid-nineteenth century. The discussion of gifts particular to specific nations was not initially race-based at all. Instead, it was the outgrowth of a branch of romantic thought that originated in the late eighteenth century. It replaced the universalist elements of Enlightenment thinking with a style of thinking that focused on the particular traits associated with particular nationalities. This romantic approach to the acceptance of difference originated in the work of the German philosopher Johann Gottfried von Herder, who saw cultural diversity as being a function of historical experience. Specifically, he saw individual national groups as being endowed with some character component that only that particular group expressed well. The emphasis on cultural relativism that characterized this romantic view of national groups became attractive both to European and American thinkers who saw that individual groups possessed both positive and negative qualities that were offset by others who possessed qualities that both complimented and contrasted. To some extent, the interest in romantic relativism was reflected in American romanticist writers like James Fenimore Cooper (especially in Natty Bumpo's thoughts on Indian "gifts" vs. the "gifts" inherent in the white race), Ralph Waldo Emerson, Nathaniel Hawthorne, and Herman Melville.

The purely romantic view of cultural diversity, with its emphasis on environmental factors, was eventually replaced by an emphasis on racial factors. The distinctions that were initially made between various ethnic groups, Germans and Anglo Saxons, for instance, were eventually replaced by a simple designation that included all of the white races. This conflation of whiteness served further to exacerbate prevailing views on black difference. Not surprisingly, many of these views found their way into views of blacks and whites and views of religion.[22] The antislave movement adopted this romantic view partially because it encouraged the acceptance of human diversity, partially because this view accommodated the abolitionist emphasis on Christian humanitarianism.

But there was also a process of idealization inherent in the abolitionist model of Christian humanitarianism. While conventional Protestant values lost their appeal for some white people, blacks were idealized by some to the point that they became symbols of oppression and virtue far beyond the realities of their existence as slaves. In the preface to *Uncle Tom's Cabin, or Life Among the Lowly* (1852), for example, Harriet Beecher Stowe articulates this attitude when she writes "The scenes of this story, as its title indicates, lie among a race hitherto ignored by the associations of polite and refined society; an exotic race, whose ancestors, born beneath a tropic sun, brought with them, and perpetrated to their descendants, a character so essentially unlike the hard and dominant Anglo-Saxon race, as for many years to have won from it only misunderstanding and contempt."[23] By basing the depiction of his life on these assumptions, Douglass shows a view of himself that is unlike the white race, of which he is, paternally speaking, at least, a part. But he is also substantially different in ideology and perspective from the black race.

IV

I have suggested these ideas as a way of introducing a revision of the way in which Chapter Ten, a chapter as central structurally as it is thematically, might be read. Chapter Ten marks the description of Douglass's yearlong stay with Edward Covey, the slave breaker, his establishment of a Sabbath school, and his ill-fated first escape attempt. The earlier scene with Aunt Hester may be read in terms of the inversion of the Noah/Ham story. The sorrow songs passage is seen in relation to Douglass's problematic relationship to the congregational-style slave singing he describes. His decision to appropriate Christian rhetoric, with all of its embedded meaning, is therefore an obvious choice for using his text to convey a depth of meaning that his story alone may not have fully conveyed. Ultimately, though, the framework upon which Douglass imposes the structure of his own story offers as many insights into some of the problems he faced in composing his narrative (and himself) as he faced in defining the needs and assumptions of his readers. What is at stake is Douglass's ability to convey meaning to his readership as well as the ability of the slave narrative form itself, which Douglass simultaneously works from within and without, adequately to convey meaning.

I say that Douglass works from both within and outside the slave narrative tradition and thereby exposes some of its inherent weaknesses because, ironically, in a chapter that centers on the beating that he claims "inspired" in him a new "determination to be free" (*N* 65), the description of the actual beating is pared down to its most essential elements and virtually rendered as a nonbeating. Douglass works in similar fashion later in the *Narrative* when he offers an elided version of the successful escape, which would have been the very element his audience eagerly anticipated. Three passages are especially important in understanding the ways in which Douglass appropriates the lan-

guage, signs, and symbols of standard Protestant Christianity and jux-
taposes them against Sandy Jenkins's African-influenced piousness.
The passage preceding the famous Covey beating scene and the extended presentation of the unsuccessful escape attempt is separated
by Douglass's establishment of the Sabbath school and a "digression"
on the inability of Christianity (or Sandy Jenkins's root) fully to serve
the needs of those who believe in them. Interestingly, each of these
passages may be characterized by the active presence of Sandy Jenkins.

Given the kind of narrative control he has exerted throughout other
areas of the narrative, Douglass is remarkably catholic in the ways in
which he assigns and changes the roles he designates those whom he
describes in this chapter. Douglass begins this period of his life lost
and wandering in the wilderness while Edward Covey is endowed
with what initially seems to be a curious mixture of omnipotently
Christ-like and sinisterly Satanic characteristics. For instance, in an
effort to keep his slaves working, ever aware of his presence, and constantly vigilant of his imminent return, Covey would sleep at odd
times and surprise his workers throughout the day: "His comings were
like a thief in the night. He appeared to us as being ever at hand" (N
57). One of several Old Testament antecedents to this image of a
"thief in the night" is Job's complaint, in which Job asserts his innocence for his increasing misfortune and equates those who fail to acknowledge God's power with "The murderer rising with the light
[who] killeth the poor and needy, and in the night is as a thief" (Job
24: 14).

While the Old Testament use of "thief in the night" imagery tends
to focus on its negative connotations, New Testament "thief" imagery
consistently revises this interpretation and tends to see it in the context of resurrection and rebirth. Christ instructs his disciples to be as
servants waiting for the return of their lord and to watch constantly
since "if the goodman of the house had known what hour the thief
would come, he would have watched, and not suffered his house to
be broken through" (Luke 12: 39). That passage immediately precedes the parable of the master who returns home to find his servant
unprepared for his return: "And that servant, which knew his lord's
will, and prepared not himself, neither did according to his will, shall
be beaten with many stripes" (Luke 12: 47). So when Covey is called
"the snake" by his slaves and described as being seen "coiled up in the
corner of the wood-fence, watching every motion of the slaves" (N
57), he assumes the ominousness of both the Old Testament thief

who is ignorant of God's will and the New Testament thief who em-
bodies the possibility of retribution for the inattentiveness of his servants. What is important here is not the derivation of a one-to-one
correlation between scriptural precedent and the rhetorical enactment
of Douglass's life, but rather to see that Douglass's own presentation
of his life as a slave, written by himself, takes on biblical authority.[24]

As Douglass explains it, "Mr. Covey's *forte* consisted of his power to
deceive. His life was devoted to planning and perpetrating the grossest
deceptions. Every thing he possessed in the shape of learning or religion, he made to conform to his disposition to deceive" (*N* 57). While
Covey, the harshest of all the slaveholding Christians described in the
Narrative, is intent on turning all things toward deception, Douglass,
his antithesis, turns all things toward a New Testament-inspired pattern of death and rebirth. Ultimately, Douglass is disclosing and interpreting the vast difference between the actual and that which merely
appears to be true. Covey had the ability to appear to his slaves to be
ever present with them and to appear to be a devoted Christian while
he was, in fact, neither of these things.

Covey insisted on a pattern of morning and evening prayer, during
which "few men . . . appear more devotional than he (*N* 57)." Douglass situates himself at Covey's moments of apparent devotion and
selectively refuses the duty of initiating the hymn. In many aspects,
Douglass's descriptions of Covey are intended to show his awareness
of the profound disparities between Christianity as it was practiced in
the South and the realities of slavery. Covey, after all, is initially described by Douglass in terms of the irony between his seeming piousness and his reputation for breaking the spirits of slaves: "Added
to the natural good qualities of Mr. Covey, he was a professor of religion—a pious soul—a member and class-leader in the Methodist
church" (*N* 54). The outward manifestation of Covey's piousness is
immediately juxtaposed against his activities on his own farm: "All
this added weight to his reputation as a 'nigger breaker' " (*N* 54).

Douglass's subsequent descriptions of Covey enlarge the disparities
between the apparent and the actual. In terms of power, if not literal
one-to-one biblical correlation, Covey serves as an individual representative of the evils inherent in southern Christianity. Covey's self-
deceptive attempts to deceive God, the empty, ritualized expression
of his religiosity, and his inability to sing hymns in anything but "the
most discordant manner" (*N* 57), is very different from the truly pious
expressions of feeling that the slaves earlier demonstrated in their sing-

ing. Furthermore, the obvious inappropriateness of a practicing Christian actively engaged in an adulterous relationship with one of his slaves is offset by Douglass's awareness of Covey's deceptions and his willingness to challenge Covey on ethical and, later, physical terms. While Covey represents the fallen church, Douglass's defiance, and by extension his defiance of slavery itself, becomes a threat to the slave system. His challenge is rooted firmly in the challenge of the Israelites to the Egyptians and the New Testament's revision of Mosaic law and Old Testament prophecy.

Douglass's challenge to Covey (and slavery) comes at his lowest physical and spiritual point. At the conclusion of his first six months with Covey, Douglass suggests that Covey had indeed been successful in breaking him: "I was broken in body, soul, and spirit. My natural elasticity was crushed, my intellect languished, the disposition to read departed, the cheerful spark that lingered about my eye died; the dark night of slavery closed in upon me; and behold a man transformed into a brute!" (*N* 58). And from this imbruted position, Douglass speaks in a hybrid language, cobbled together from his own experiences of secular conversion (that is, conversion from a brute to a man) rendered in the traditional language of a religious conversion. And, appropriately, that secular conversion rendered in nonsecular terms has its origins on the Sabbath in a hybrid state "between sleep and wake" (*N* 58).

His famous apostrophe to the Chesapeake, in which he pours out his desire for freedom in a Job-like complaint to the Almighty, reinforces the framework of religious language and imagery that Douglass openly draws upon while simultaneously offering an indirect representation of the route he eventually uses for escape.[25] But Douglass's secular conversion also indicates what may be seen as an unwillingness on Douglass's part fully to give over the credit for his secular conversion to the benevolent God to whom he speaks. Unlike the pattern of many slave narratives, he fails to include a specific scene of conversion in his narrative. The *Narrative* even goes so far as to suggest, especially with the problematic insertion of Sandy Jenkins's root into Douglass's recitation of the turning point of his life as a slave, that Christianity is insufficient for the task of overthrowing an unjust slave system so thoroughly ensconced in Christian rhetoric.

In a very un-Christian-like stance, Douglass even goes so far as openly to doubt the existence of God ("Is there any God?" [*N* 59]). But unlike the kinds of complaints put forth by Job and David, Doug-

lass is unwilling to place his fate in the hands of a God who allows one
of His children to be enslaved. Instead, Douglass takes on the burden
of his own secular salvation ("I will run away. I will not stand it. Get
caught or get clear, I'll try it. I had as well die with ague as the fever.
I have only one life to lose. I had as well be killed running as die
standing" [N 59]). Douglass questions, though he seems unwilling
fully to deny, God's power. Later, he questions, though fails fully to
deny, the power of the root Sandy offers him. If Douglass is not completely convinced of God's attention, he is eventually reborn into the
spirit of rebellion and self-determinance. The spiritual death he described earlier is temporary. But his rebirth, though rendered in religious terms, is largely self-determined and secular.[26]

His apostrophe to the Chesapeake begins as a religiously inspired
secular vision. The ships, moving freely in and out of the harbor, become angelic representations of freedom and escape: "You are freedom's swift-winged angels, that fly round the world; I am confined in
bands of iron! . . . The glad ship is gone; she hides in the dim distance.
I am left in the hottest hell of unending slavery" (N 59). Douglass is
ultimately able to end this passage, which describes his period of deepest spiritual death, with a profound moment of hope and rebirth ("It
may be that my misery in slavery will only increase my happiness when
I get free. There is a better day coming" [N 60]).

It should therefore come as no surprise to his reader that Douglass
is able to balance the inexorable death that characterized his first eight
months with Covey against the rebirth that characterized the final
third of the year in the brief sentence that serves as the thematic pivot
point of the chapter: "You have seen how a man was made a slave; you
shall see how a slave was made a man" (N 60). It is not an account of
transfiguration, like Saul's conversion on the road to Damascus, or
Augustine's account of living a depraved secular life before being res-
cued from the depths of his depravity by a loving, forgiving God.
Instead, Douglass's transfiguration from beastial slave to freeman is
largely self-directed and, except in the way it is rendered, apparently
has relatively little to do with religious conversion. But there is a
strong theological component to this pivotal chapter in which Douglass places himself in a miscegenated position between his African her-
itage and the dominant ideas of the culture in which he lives. If Protestant Christianity frames one side of this position, then the providential
appearance of Sandy Jenkins and his root serves as the other side of
the frame.

In referring to his narratee as "you," and therefore virtually negat-
ing the distance between the actual reader of the text and the implied
person to whom the text is narrated, Douglass seems to be suggesting
that the only way one can understand the importance of his experiences is through the text itself. One is drawn within the circle of oppression through Douglass's rhetorical skills alone. But "voice" is
tightly bound up with the gaze. As with W.E.B. Du Bois, who becomes aware of his "doubleness" through the disparaging gaze of his
classmate, the eventual attainment of "voice" requires, for Douglass,
an awareness and manipulation of the reader. The reader, through
the act of reading, becomes as inscribed and encircled by the text as
Douglass indicates he was by his condition as a slave. Douglass's interest in creating this narratee is not to facilitate engagement (as Harriet
Jacobs's creation of her own narratee implies) but to encourage the
development of the narratee's vision so that the culturally constructed
divisions between Douglass's experiences and his readers' reaction to
those experiences could be minimized and ultimately eliminated.[27]

As Douglass tells it, his transformation from beast to man began at
3:00 in the afternoon on one of the hottest days of the hottest months.
After spending the entire day fanning wheat with three others, Douglass was overcome by the heat and unable to continue work. Covey,
who was only 100 yards or so away, heard the fan stop, came to inquire
why work had ceased, and found Douglass prostrate beneath the rail
of a fence. Covey beat Douglass and bloodied his head, at which point
Douglass decided he would return to his owner, Thomas Auld (see
Illustration 3.5), in hopes of receiving some kind of protection.
Douglass's trip through the woods turned him into a kind of nineteenth-century Jeremiah: "From the crown of my head to my feet, I
was covered with blood. My hair was all clotted with dust and blood;
my shirt was stiff with blood. My legs and feet were torn in sundry
places with briers and thorns, and were also covered with blood. I
suppose I looked like a man who had escaped a den of wild beasts,
and barely escaped them" (N 62).

Though undoubtedly surprised by Douglass's unexpected reappear-
ance, Thomas Auld sent Douglass back to Covey with the threat of a
further beating if he did not go. (Auld, after all, had essentially leased
Douglass to Covey for the entire year in hopes that Covey would accomplish exactly that which he was achieving, which was to "break"
Douglass.) Douglass thus "started off to Covey's in the morning, (Saturday morning,) wearied in body and broken in spirit" (N 62). Doug-

Illustration 3.5. Daguerreotype of Frederick Douglass's owner, Thomas Auld. Unidentified photographer. Courtesy of Mrs. William Sears.

lass spent the day mostly hiding from Covey, who intended to beat him in retribution for running away, before he "fell in with Sandy Jenkins" (*N* 63), a fellow slave with whom he was acquainted. Like Thomas Auld, Sandy told him "with great solemnity," that he must return to Covey. But Sandy dispatches Douglass with a root that he insists will serve as a talisman against another beating by Covey, provided Douglass remembers always to carry it on his right side.

So, in the midst of a series of Protestant Christian representations, Douglass inserts an attachment to the African "root" that metaphorically reconnects him to his origins. And on the Sunday that Douglass returns to Covey, the root, in conjunction with the sabbath, seems to serve its purpose. Covey simply pauses on his way to church and instructs Douglass to work on the relatively easy task of driving pigs: "Now, this singular conduct of Mr. Covey really made me begin to think that there was something in the *root* which Sandy had given me; and had it been on any other day than Sunday, I could have attributed the conduct to no other cause than the influence of that root; and as it was, I was half inclined to think the *root* to be something more than I at first had taken it to be" (*N* 63).

There is a strong argument to be made for seeing Douglass as explicitly questioning the ability of Sandy's root to serve as an adequate remedy for slavery. Or perhaps Douglass is urging his reader to question any singular ideology that is not directly connected to individual action.[28] Either way, in Douglass's presentation of the event, resistance made incarnate in physical violence was the deciding factor. These elements work in conjunction with the element of surprise and individual action that is part of Douglass's reprisal and makes its success much more than the result of a simple appropriation of either Judeo-Christian or African forms.

Ultimately, in a.large sense the entire narrative functions not only because Douglass is able to appropriate Judeo-Christian and African forms, but because he is able selectively to utilize aspects of those forms to give his particular narrative universal meaning. Douglass, for instance, is unable fully to appropriate the Judeo-Christian form. Covey is not completely satanic. Douglass is not completely messianic. No religiously inspired conversion takes place. His departure on Friday afternoon after his "death" at 3:00 does not culminate on Sunday morning with his "rebirth."[29] The root itself is equally suspect. He is, after all, only "half" inclined to consider the root's power. The other half of his inclination is that his brief interaction with Covey on his way to church may have mitigated Covey's physical retribution.

The construction of the text places in the background the physicality of his confrontation with Covey on Monday morning; the description of the fight itself is remarkably brief. Douglass writes that "I resolved to fight; and, suiting my action to the resolution, I seized Covey hard by the throat; and as I did so, I rose. He held on to me, and I to him. My resistance was so entirely unexpected, that Covey seemed taken all aback. He trembled like a leaf" (*N* 64). Douglass's unexpected physical violence contributes much more to the cause of his success than Sandy's root. Covey responds as much to the unexpectedness of Douglass's singular response as he does to its physicality. Furthermore, Douglass does not go so far as to suggest that either the root or Christianity ("from whence came the spirit I don't know" [*N* 64]), separately or in combination, adequately addresses his needs. The confrontation with Covey is enacted in a physical confrontation, but that confrontation also speaks toward the individualized, hybrid space that Douglass has narratologically created for himself.

In the representation of the fight with Covey that he gives in the *Narrative*, Douglass suggests that his battle is entirely singular and based on his physical response to Covey. Covey calls for assistance from a hired man named Bill who declines on the grounds that his master hired him out to work and not to help Covey fight his battles with Frederick. After Bill's apparent departure, Douglass writes that "We [Douglass and Covey] were at it for nearly two hours" (*N* 64). No one else is mentioned in the context of the moment. "Covey at length let me go, puffing and blowing at a great rate, saying that if I had not resisted, he would not have whipped me half so much. The truth was, that he had not whipped me at all. I considered him as getting entirely the worst end of the bargain; for he had drawn no blood from me, but I had from him" (*N* 65). And true to that miscegenated space, Douglass is able to claim the influence and authority of two apparently unreconcilable worldviews. In the physical expression of these two authorizing systems for his actions, he experiences the kind of transubstantiation that is the true turning point of the narrative: "I felt as I never felt before. It was a glorious resurrection, from the tomb of slavery, to the heaven of freedom" (*N* 65).[30]

In a Christian context, the true meaning of Christ's death is inscribed in his rebirth on the morning of the third day. Similarly, the true meaning of Douglass's metaphorical death occurs at the point of his figurative rebirth. After all, if Douglass had been successfully "broken" by Covey, he would simply have been one of the many slaves who experienced a similar fate because of Covey and others like him. What sets Douglass's recitation of the experience apart from other recitations of the story is that Douglass experienced the "rebirth" that allowed him to transcend the experience.

Having completed his description of death and resurrection, Douglass offers several general critiques of aspects of the slave system. He specifically focuses on the holidays between Christmas and New Year's Day, where slaves are encouraged to abuse their relative freedom in hopes of disgusting themselves to the entire idea of true freedom, and examines the ways in which the slave system uses religion to justify and obscure its inhumanity. This eventually leads to a description of his decision, while a slave on the plantation of Mr. Freeland, to clandestinely establish a Sabbath school. It is here that Sandy Jenkins, who is also one of Mr. Freeland's hired slaves, reappears in the *Narrative*. His involvement in this passage, as in the preceding passage in which he offers Douglass the root, is as unsettled (and unsettling) as it is in the subsequent description of his connection to Douglass's failed escape attempt. But his association with these three important passages in the central chapter of the *Narrative* is worth examining in some detail.

To a large extent, the very inclusion of Sandy as a foil for Douglass indicates some of the issues Douglass must reconcile in the rhetorical creation of himself. That self-creation seeks to combine the fictions of form associated with the relationship of his own individual, miscegenated rebellion to the kind of rebellion represented by explicit connection to a more "authentic" African American.[31] Sandy, after all, provides Douglass with the root that metaphorically grounds him to African religious and folkloric traditions. The root serves as a force against which the Christian tradition could be examined and implicitly called into question. Sandy's relatively positive influence in his initial appearance is followed by a relatively neutral appearance before being transfigured into the unseen force that seems to betray the escape attempt. But to view Sandy merely as Douglass's foil, as his Peter at Gethsemane, or his Judas at the Last Supper, implies for Douglass a position that he does not seem to be fully seeking for himself.

The *Narrative* takes for its uses the authority of Christian language and occurrence, thus "authorizing" the paradoxical position of an escaped slave legitimizing himself in a social context that did not otherwise recognize his legitimacy. After wondering whether or not Sandy's root may have had some influence in initially protecting him from Covey, Douglass goes on to subvert any reading of the *Narrative* that would fully connect that partial salvation with the root any more than allow that salvation to be connected to traditional Protestant theology. If the relationship between the two was initially hinted at in Sandy's first appearance, the association of either of these modes of salvation is ultimately undercut in Sandy's second appearance. There, Douglass adds a footnote criticizing those who seek to believe that kind of illogical thinking: "We used frequently to talk about the fight with Covey, and as often as we did so, he [Sandy] would claim my success as the result of the roots which he gave me. This superstition is very common among the more ignorant slaves. A slave seldom dies but that his death is attributed to trickery" (*N* 70).

Lest the reader think that Douglass's critique of Sandy's root implies even a partial endorsement of Christianity, what Douglass has to say about the Sabbath school he organizes to teach literacy does away with any kind of mistaken assumptions. His emphasis here is especially noteworthy because while he underscores the fact that he is using the Bible to teach reading, there is no indication that his interest is theological in any way. The Bible is simply the literary vehicle around which he organizes his lessons: "It was necessary to keep our religious masters at St. Michael's unacquainted with the fact, that, . . ., we were trying to learn how to read the will of God" (*N* 71). The distinction here is subtle but important. The emphasis, both in terms of why Douglass is originally persuaded to organize the Sabbath school and what he sees as his mission within that context, is on literacy rather than religious training. This is completely compatible with his use of religion throughout the *Narrative* as a way of establishing meaning and establishing himself as the conveyer and interpreter of that meaning.

Douglass's narrative position, as well as the *Narrative*'s framing documents, reinforces the fact that the cruel schoolhouse of experience that Douglass encounters as a slave functions on the concept of denying knowledge. Since his conception of the denial of knowledge runs both ways, Douglass is able to write a narrative defined as much by the denial of knowledge (his age, his parentage, literacy, the meaning of the slave songs, the exact particulars of his escape) as by its acquisition (the Aunt Hester beating passage, his triumph over Covey, his acquisition of literacy and "voice") and his self-conscious presentation of that knowledge to his readership in the form of the text itself.[32] As with his relationship to the slaves he instructs at his Sabbath school, Douglass's delight is enlightening: "They came because they wished to learn. Their minds had been starved by their cruel masters. They had been shut up in mental darkness. I taught them, because it was the delight of my soul to be doing something that looked like bettering the condition of my race" (N 71–72).

The emphasis on bettering the race again moves Douglass to the point of blasphemy when he claims that he was "almost" ready to ask " 'Does a righteous God govern the universe? and for what does he hold the thunders in his right hand, if not to smite the oppressor, and deliver the spoiled out of the hand of the spoiler?' " (N 71). Thus, after censuring Sandy's root as meaningless superstition and criticizing the Christian God for inaction, Douglass chooses an alternate course of action when he says "My course was upward. . . . These thoughts roused me—I must do something" (N 72). The emphasis, as in his physical response to Covey, is on individual physical action rather than on waiting for a larger system of invisible kindness and mercy.

Having seen the ways in which Douglass introduces Sandy at other crucial points in this chapter, how are we to read Sandy's relationship to the failed escape attempt? Douglass writes that though he was careful about those with whom he confided—those within the circle—it was important for him to formulate his escape with them rather than simply engineer his own escape. Sandy, though, seems to have gotten cold feet at the last moment ("Sandy . . . gave up the notion but still encouraged us" [N 74]) and the *Narrative* implies that it was Sandy who informed on the group. Douglass's moment of awareness, like Nat Turner's, occurs in the field, where he announces to Sandy his realization of betrayal, to which Sandy enigmatically replies " 'Well, . . . , that thought has this moment struck me' " (N 76). These are Sandy's final words before receding from the *Narrative*, but they seem especially prescient. Later, after the group was captured, Douglass writes that "We found the evidence against us to be the testimony of one person; our master would not tell us who it was; but we came to a unanimous decision among ourselves as to who the informant was" (N 78).[33]

Sandy's apparent giving over of his fellow slaves seems to indicate that the limitation of the root to which Douglass earlier alluded may also be applied to the limitations of cultural rootedness. If Sandy whom, after all, Douglass portrays as being more connected to the African folk tradition than he, can step outside of the circle and betray his fellow slaves, then the path to freedom that Douglass seeks requires the same kind of individual initiative and action for success that his confrontation with Covey implies. (In keeping with this idea, it is worth noting that Douglass's actual escape was singular and did not benefit a group.) Douglass's decision to write a series of passes for the group, which he calls "protections," intended to mask the movements of the group while on the Baltimore Bay, authenticates their movement to those who might inquire about it in much the same way the *Narrative* authenticates and justifies for his reading audience Douglass's own rhetorical movements.

As such, Douglass's *Narrative* represents a double act of self-creation, embodied in one respect in the act of escape as a creation of the self outside of slavery and in another respect in Douglass's decision to write the story of his escape. He was now free from slavery (though not necessarily of the effects of slavery or other forms of racism) and free rhetorically to recreate the events of his life. However, he did all of this in addition to creating himself out of the encircling boundaries of the Garrisonian abolitionism that first gave him a platform for the expression of his "voice." Through the agency of Garrisonian abolitionism, Douglass would have his reader believe that he initially found the language to critique slavery and America and subsequently realized the limitations of the very institution that first gave him that platform. Ironically, in the same way former slaves took language and transformed it into something slaveholders never intended, Douglass was able to take the language of Garrisonian abolitionism (which itself drew heavily on Protestant religious discourse) and transform it into something abolitionists never intended. His *Narrative* clearly points toward a synthetic representation of the various personae the *Narrative* required him to occupy: Slave, fugitive slave, antislavery lecturer, writer, and established political figure.

4

Authority, Power, and Determination of the Will: The Dilemma of Rhetorical Ownership in Frederick Douglass's *My Bondage and My Freedom* and Harriet Jacobs's *Incidents in the Life of a Slave Girl*

> I am telling you the plain truth.
> —Harriet Jacobs, *Incidents in the Life of a Slave Girl*

THE AFRICAN American social and cultural identity that is rhetorically constructed in the fugitive slave narrative form may be seen in terms of the stolen words that African Americans took and endowed with their own meanings, as Richard Wright described the process. It may similarly be seen in terms of Bakhtin's complimentary thoughts on the ways in which social identities are constructed out of the language used to describe that experience. In these contexts, Frederick Douglass's *My Bondage and My Freedom* (1855) and Harriet Jacobs's *Incidents in the Life of a Slave Girl* (1861) (hereafter *Incidents*) offer valuable insights into the tensions inherent in reconciling the various and competing modes of discourse available to them. My interest in bringing these narratives together is to address the issue of who it is who actually controls the narrative. It seems to me that the separation of narrative "voice" from narrative subject and the insistence by the narrative "voice" of control over its rhetorical product represents a kind of victory by the slave narrator that anticipates the "gift of second sight" that Du Bois proposes in *The Souls of Black Folk*. In one respect, the "second sight" to which Du Bois refers indicates the limitation in how the stories of slave narrators were interpreted and understood. But in another equally important sense, the "gift" imparted by "second sight" is an awareness of the "doubleness" implicit in the rhetorical creation of an African American social identity. In this chapter, I will address the ways each of these narratives examines the issue of authority and how the texts seek to resolve the precarious positions of subjectivity and objectivity that the narrators, as the writers of their stories and the experiencers of their stories, are simultaneously forced to assume. Specifically, my interest is to read these texts in relation to a larger context of narrative economy and to see them as offering an analysis of the literary pressures encountered by slave narrators within the rhetorical possibilities available to them.

I

In *My Bondage and My Freedom*, which Douglass used to revise and expand his *Narrative* ten years after its publication, the fundamental questions continue to be: Who controls the telling and interpretation of the story? And what is the context (rhetorical and cultural) that lends authority to the "voice" telling the story? The earlier narrative concerned itself with the issue of finding a "voice." As the encircling structure of the text suggests, that "voice" is very much a function of the enabling presence of William Lloyd Garrison and the antislavery agenda that was authorized by the appropriation of biblical language and event. Clearly, though, that issue was not adequately resolved for Douglass, who sought to reauthorize the writerly "voice" that the earlier narrative sought so diligently to produce. The earlier narrative was concerned with appropriating and correctly responding to the needs and, more importantly, the expectations of his audience. The second narrative dispenses with many of those concerns and focuses considerably less on Douglass's experiences as a slave (a representative slave, but a slave nonetheless) and instead devotes its attention to the pressures he faced as an individual as he become a public figure (see Illustration 4.1).

As one might imagine, in the broadest sense, the overall structure of the areas of overlap between *My Bondage and My Freedom* and the *Narrative* are remarkably similar. But *My Bondage and My Freedom* is far more than simply an expanded version of the earlier narrative. It tells a different story altogether. The most obvious revisionary technique that Douglass employs throughout is not only to expand the

Illustration 4.1. Daguerreotype of Frederick Douglass in his thirties. Unidentified photographer, circa 1850 after 1847 daguerreotype. National Portrait Gallery, Smithsonian Institution, Washington, D.C.

details of particular passages but on several occasions to expand the
roles of people in those passages. While the earlier *Narrative* presents
a presence thoroughly individualized (and seemingly isolated, in many
ways), *My Bondage and My Freedom* is considerably more careful to
reorient Douglass's experiences within a larger framework of black
connection. The binary stance suggested by the theme and structure
of *My Bondage and My Freedom* is deceptively simplistic. What Henry
Louis Gates refers to as "binary oppositions" only tells part of the
story. A more complete version is revealed through the interaction of
a series of simultaneously competing oppositions.[1] At an important
turning point in the *Narrative*, Douglass writes that "You have seen
how a man was made a slave; you shall see how a slave was made a
man" (*N* 60). *My Bondage and My Freedom* redefines that dichotomy
by examining the ways in which the man developed in the *Narrative*
developed himself into a great man.

If Douglass has indeed initially created a text in which his objective
was to find a "voice" and then chosen to redefine that text with the
objective of using that authorizing "voice" to create himself as a subject, then the methods available to him for achieving that goal are
disturbing and, in many ways, extraordinarily unsatisfying.[2] *My Bondage and My Freedom* is characterized by Douglass's decision to expand
and develop certain passages (like the first escape sequence), incorporate verbatim passages from the *Narrative* (like the slave songs area),
and add to that framework various examples of his work as a public
figure (like speeches and newspaper clippings). He also selectively
chooses to deepen his appropriation of religious language and imagery, thus suggesting that his ability to recreate himself in the revised
narrative is more precarious than the apparent confidence *My Bondage
and My Freedom* suggests. The revised narrative encompasses and interprets the experiences of the earlier narrative in the same way that
Garrison's voice encircles and interprets that narrative. To some extent, *My Bondage and My Freedom* replaces Douglass's disengagement
with Garrisonian abolitionism (rather than his fight with Covey) as
his inevitable moment of self-articulation.[3] This is true to the extent
that in *My Bondage and My Freedom* the battle with Covey enriches
the description of his experiences with Garrisonian abolitionism by
casting those descriptions in a new light. Arguably, his expanded description of the confrontation with Edward Covey speaks toward
Douglass's realization that in facing and defeating the most evil of the
slave breakers, who represents the most evil and repressive aspects of

the slave system, Douglass would have the physical and emotional tools necessary to resist all subsequent assaults on his individuality.

The revision process begins taking place in the prefatory material of the narrative when the endorsement of the black abolitionist James McCune alone replaces the endorsements that were earlier provided by William Lloyd Garrison and Wendell Phillips. But McCune engages and challenges, both directly and indirectly, the ideas that Garrison has earlier presented. At the very outset, for instance, McCune refutes Garrison's earlier estimation of Douglass and revises Garrison's understanding of the abolitionist movement by writing "The life of Frederick Douglass, recorded in the pages which follow, is not merely an example of self-elevation under the most adverse circumstances; it is, moreover, a noble vindication of the highest aims of the American anti-slavery movement. The real object of that movement is not only to disenthrall, it is, also, to bestow upon the negro the exercise of all those rights, from the possession of which he has been so long debarred."[4] McCune is correct in calling *My Bondage and My Freedom* a "noble vindication" of what the antislavery movement professed to believe. In a subtle but important revision of the first narrative, *My Bondage and My Freedom* equates Garrison's antislavery movement as much with control as with the sovereign opportunity the movement initially appears to convey.

Douglass endows the initial moments of his escape in New Bedford with the church. As the title of the book suggests, his initial confrontation with organized religion is constrained and unsatisfactory. This eventually leads Douglass rhetorically to take on the true meaning of Christianity and apply it to his antislavery activities. The religiosity and spiritual commitment that Douglass expects to find in the Methodist church turns out to be false; the antislavery movement (initially, at least) takes on descriptive qualities that the church was unable to sustain. During the minister's administration of the sacrament to the African-American members of the Elm Street church, Douglass observes the disgraceful way they are treated and notes that "During the whole ceremony, they looked like sheep without a shepherd" (*MBMF* 361). Douglass, during his brief membership in a congregation of African-American Methodists almost seems to be suggesting that he himself is a kind of shepherd to the flock: "Favored with the affection and confidence of the members of this humble communion, I was soon made a class-leader and a local preacher among them. Many seasons of peace and joy I experienced among them, the remembrance of which is still precious, although I could not see it to be my duty to remain with that body, when I found that it consented to the same spirit which held my brethren in chains" (*MBMF* 361–62). In the sort of cyclic theme and variation that characterizes the book, Douglass looks from sacred salvation and leadership to a secularized version of salvation that he saturates with all the energy, possibility, and passion of a revealed religious experience.

Douglass's secular conversion occurs when he is approached by an abolitionist agent about subscribing to *The Liberator*, which soon "took its place with [him] next to the bible" and became "a paper after [his] own heart" (*MBMF* 362). A series of religious correspondences serve to highlight the reasons Douglass was drawn to Garrisonian abolitionism in the first place. This, to a large degree, is the primary function of religion in the narrative.[5] But this passage, and subsequent passages, further serves to engage the reader in the larger quest in which Douglass found himself. Passages like this double as intellectual and emotional arguments intended to ground Douglass's experiences and reactions to a larger course of meaning and significance.

In *My Bondage and My Freedom*, Douglass expands his time with Edward Covey into three chapters. This sequence begins with Douglass connecting his psychic landscape to the bleakness of the New Year's Day of 1834, "with its chilling wind and pinching frost," which he found "quite in harmony with the winter in my own mind" (*MBMF* 258). Even the exterior landscape reinforces his sense of bleakness and barrenness: "The Chesapeake bay [upon which Covey's house stood] deepened the wild and desolate aspect of my new home" (*MBMF* 259). Chapter Fifteen (entitled "Covey, the Negro Breaker") is the first chapter describing Douglass's initial six months with Covey. It largely incorporates descriptions of the beatings and the overall harshness of the situation and concludes with a verbatim insertion of the apostrophe to the Chesapeake that Douglass described in the *Narrative*.

The primary point of augmentation in this passage is Douglass's expansion of the scene in which he is required by Covey to use two unbroken oxen to collect wood from the forest, which was about two miles from the farm. Douglass skillfully uses this passage to identify the oxen with a series of contexts. Consistent with Covey's role as the person who introduces Douglass most fully to his status as a slave and to the possibility of lifelong servitude, it is Covey who introduces

Douglass to the oxen: "In due form, and with all proper ceremony, I was introduced to this huge yoke of unbroken oxen. . . . The master of this important ceremony was no less a person than Mr. Covey, himself" (*MBMF* 260–61). Douglass, in his first experiences as a field hand, is initially confused and misreads the situation by wondering why there is any need to differentiate between what seems to him to be two completely identical things. Though he "was carefully told which was 'Buck,' and which was 'Darby'—which was the 'in hand,' and which was the 'off hand' ox," he cannot help wondering "Where and what is the reason for this distinction in names, when there is none in the things themselves?" (*MBMF* 261).

What Douglass subsequently realizes, though, is that while he "knew no more of oxen, than the driver is supposed to know of wisdom" (*MBMF* 262), his connection to the oxen is more organic and significant than either he or the reader might imagine: "Tame and docile to a proverb, when *well* trained, the ox is the most sullen and intractable of animals when but half broken to the yoke. I now saw, in my situation, several points of similarity with that of the oxen. They were property, so was I; they were to be broken, so was I. Covey was to break me, I was to break them; break and be broken—such is life" (*MBMF* 263). In equating himself with the oxen as Covey's property to be broken in the natural order of things, Douglass notes, in what wryly foreshadows his experiences with Garrisonian abolitionists "in passing, that working animals in the south, are seldom so well trained as in the north" (*MBMF* 260).

In a narrative as concerned with reading and interpretation as it is with writing, Douglass presents an example of his own inability to read a situation (initially, at least) and, in passing, offers a veiled reference to his eventual status as abolitionist "property" and to the fact that, ironically, abolitionist sponsors trained their beasts of burden considerably more efficiently than those they apparently opposed. Douglass's initial confusion about how "things" that appeared to be exactly the same and that seemingly shared identical functions mirrors the inability of slaveholders and abolitionists alike to see blacks as anything beyond the stereotyped roles they are obligated to play. After having described himself in direct relation to Covey's oxen (after his inability properly to control the ox cart), Douglass writes that he is subjected to a beating from Covey with the branches of a black gum tree, which were commonly called ox-goads because of their strength and usefulness in driving ox.

Douglass modifies the description of his turning point on Covey's farm in a way that deemphasizes the previous beastial description in favor of one that emphasizes the reader's role in properly interpreting the significance of Douglass's experience: "You have, dear reader, seen me humbled, degraded, broken down, enslaved, and brutalized, and you understand how it was done; now let us see the converse of all this, and how it was brought about" (*MBMF* 270). In order to ensure that his reader properly understands how that transformation took place, Douglass expands the stark presentation he employed in the earlier narrative in favor of a more detailed description of the experience.

Douglass has already shown how he himself, one who has experienced the realities of slavery firsthand, initially proved to be an imperfect reader of his own experience. Upon escaping from Covey and returning bloodied and scarred to his owner, Thomas Auld, Douglass presents another failed reader. Douglass writes that Auld initially responded very sympathetically to his experiences. But that initial human connection to the predicament of another was quickly replaced with the standard response of the slaveowner: "At first, master Thomas seemed somewhat affected by the story of my wrongs, but he soon repressed his feelings and became cold as iron" (*MBMF* 275). As evidence that the slave system exterminates the humanity of all who come in contact with it (Mrs. Auld was another person whose humanity was extinguished when Douglass describes in the *Narrative* the change she underwent after being told by her husband to stop teaching young Frederick to read), Captain Auld demands that Douglass return to Covey early the next morning. His argument is that if Douglass should return from Covey without fulfilling the agreement that he remain there for the entire year, Auld would lose Douglass's wages for the remainder of the year. As Douglass realizes, even his position as Auld's property was compromised: "My master, who I did not venture to hope would protect me as *a man*, had even now refused to protect me as *his property*" (*MBMF* 277).

When Douglass returns to Covey's farm on Saturday morning, he makes reference to Covey's "snakish habits." But unlike the earlier recitation of this passage, Douglass is not at this point fully degraded in his own mind to the bestial. The distinction is this: In the earlier version, Douglass indicates that Covey was able fully to rob from Douglass his humanity, which Douglass reclaimed in his confrontation with Covey. In the recitation of the story in *My Bondage and My*

Freedom, Douglass's point seems to be a bit more subtle. Douglass suggests that he has descended to the level of the beastial because that is the only way adequately to confront Covey. In a system that reduces and dehumanizes all who encounter it, the only way to exist as equals is to accept the beastial.[6] But before the expanded confrontation with Covey, Douglass offers his encounter with Sandy Jenkins, whose entrance and presence is also expanded beyond its initial confines in the *Narrative*.

The earlier *Narrative* relentlessly placed Douglass as an individual figure in conflict with a larger collective experience. Douglass's individuality was emphasized to the point that even his wife Anna Murray's role in his eventual escape was eliminated in the larger description of Douglass's accomplishment. Here, Douglass's singularity is apparently mitigated by the fact that Sandy both figuratively (in the sense that he offers Douglass access to the African tradition via the root) and literally (in his invitation to Douglass to return to Sandy's wife's house for food and shelter, even at the risk of severe physical punishment if Douglass was discovered) provides Douglass with communal connection. This is one of the relatively few instances where Douglass places his own experience in the context of a larger framework of African-American encouragement and support.[7]

Yet, beyond the intrinsic good nature of the support he receives from other African Americans, their aid to Douglass, at least in terms of the way he describes it, was very much a function of their acknowledgment and respect for his unique position in slave society: "Sandy's wife was not behind him in kindness—both seemed to esteem it a privilege to succor me; for, although I was hated by Covey and by my master, I was loved by the colored people, because *they* thought I was hated for my knowledge, and persecuted because I was feared. I was the *only* slave *now* in that region who could read and write" (*MBMF* 279–80). Though he uses this scene to foreshadow the singularity of his experience and accomplishment, Douglass is also able to create for himself a paternal foundation in the figure of Sandy Jenkins. Sandy provides Douglass a more specific connection to the black community, foreshadows his eventual break with Garrisonian abolitionism, and looks toward his deeper engagement with black antislavery figures like Henry Highland Garnet and Samuel R. Ward. This is not to suggest that Douglass blindly agreed with African-American abolitionism. Indeed, Douglass and Garnet had a lifelong ideological disagreement with one another. Douglass's involvement with black abolitionists seems to have contributed to important changes in his political thought, like his reading of the Constitution as an antislavery document and his willingness to endorse violent slave resistance. This shift in opinion may also account for the brevity of the description of Douglass's battle with Covey in the *Narrative* and its revision and expansion in *My Bondage and My Freedom*.[8]

In my discussion of the *Narrative*, I commented on the way in which Sandy's presentation of the root to Douglass served as a kind of antithesis to Douglass's critique of Christianity, especially in relation to his eventual emphasis on his individual action in defeating Covey. Yet in *My Bondage and My Freedom*, Sandy and Douglass actively discuss Douglass's options before Sandy suggests to him the root, which Douglass says is based upon "a system for which I have no name" (*MBMF* 280). Douglass's inability adequately to give words to Sandy's system suggests for Sandy a subordinate significance that betrays Douglass's ability rhetorically to define and control his environment. Douglass writes that "It was beneath one of my intelligence to countenance such dealings with the devil, as this power implied. But, with all my learning—it was really precious little—Sandy was more than a match for me. 'My book learning,' he said, 'had not kept Covey off me,' (a powerful argument just then,) and he entreated me, with flashing eyes, to try this" (*MBMF* 281).

Douglass's reintegration into a community of thought and practice reflects the enlarged communal arena in which the fight itself takes place. In the *Narrative*, Douglass writes that he and Covey fought alone for nearly two hours, interrupted briefly by Covey's cousin Hughes and Bill, a slave owned by Samuel Harris, to whom Covey called for assistance. In the revised rehearsal of the incident, Hughes and Bill are still present. Caroline, one of Covey's slaves, is added to the scene. Covey first asks Bill for help, then Caroline. She, like Bill, declines. Douglass's description of Caroline as being "a powerful woman" who could have very easily "mastered" (*MBMF* 285) him provides her with a strength in direct contrast to her status as Covey's slave. Caroline becomes Douglass's counterpart in both her physical strength and the fact that she is beholden to Covey's good will: "But, poor Caroline, like myself, was at the mercy of the merciless Covey; nor did she escape the dire effects of her refusal. He gave her several sharp blows" (*MBMF* 285). Her presence additionally underscores the fact that Douglass is acting with (and in reaction to) a series of enlarged cultural contexts that were largely absent from the *Narrative*. Preceding the fight, for instance, Douglass resolves to "obey every order, however unreasonable, if it were possible"(*MBMF* 282) (that is, to essentially invoke the Christian principle of turning the other cheek), and "if Mr. Covey should then undertake to beat me, to defend and protect myself to the best of my ability" (*MBMF* 282). By invoking and combining the Christian principles of humility and self-sacrifice with active physical resistance (possibly inspired by Sandy's root), Douglass enlarges the context in which he initially placed his actions in the *Narrative*.[9]

Sandy Jenkins's dreams begin as Douglass and his group make preparations for what will be their failed escape attempt. Like the root, the dreams are presented in terms of the African folk tradition from which they arise. And Douglass again plays them within a Christian context suggesting that the Christian stories of prophecy they resemble are as unfounded as Sandy's dreams. The dream that Douglass finds most disturbing resembles the kind of apocalyptically rendered prophecy that appears in both Revelation and Nat Turner's *Confessions*. According to Douglass, Sandy said that

> I dreamed, last night, that I was roused from sleep by strange noises, like the voices of a swarm of angry birds, that caused a roar as they passed, which fell upon my ear like a coming gale over the tops of the trees. Looking up to see what it could mean . . . I saw you, Frederick, in the claws of a huge bird, surrounded by a large number of birds, of all colors and sizes. These were all picking at you, while you, with your arms, seemed to be trying to protect your eyes. Passing over me, the birds flew in a south-westerly direction, and I watched them until they were clean out of sight. Now I saw this as plainly as I now see you; and furder, honey, watch de Friday night dream; dare is sumpon in it, shose you born; dare is, indeed, honey" (*MBMF* 312–13).

Given Sandy's beliefs in the protective powers of the root he has instructed Douglass to carry in order to avoid being beaten by Covey, it is not clear whether his dream should be read as a folklorically inspired prophecy or as a kind of Christian apocalyptic vision. Perhaps the blurring of distinction between the two is intentional on Douglass's part and is to be read as his subverting the true power of the vision while simultaneously taking for his own use the authority inscribed in its language.

While Sandy's dream directly prophecies the events of the escape, it simultaneously offers indirect prophecy of Douglass's "escape" from his abolitionist supporters. This subsequent "escape" also centered around the question of textual interpretation and, more specifically, the question of who, given the constraints of audience expectations, controlled the interpretation of the text. Though Douglass is disturbed by the apparent meaning of the dream, he is able to find an alternate interpretation ("by attributing it to the general excitement and perturbation consequent upon our contemplated plan of escape" [*MBMF* 313]) that allows him to discount its apparent meaning.

The passage eventually doubles back upon itself and allows Douglass the opportunity to reinterpret (or at least revise) his earlier explanation. Douglass's realization that his group had been betrayed reveals itself to him in a prophetic reworking of Nat Turner's prophetic vision in the field when Turner realizes his own messianic role: "While thus engaged, I had a sudden presentiment, which flashed upon me like lightning in a dark night, revealing to the lonely traveler the gulf before, and the enemy behind" (*MBMF* 316). The prophetically inspired rhetorical style combined with its secular application ultimately leads to the passes Douglass has forged for the group. Much has been made of those passes, but Douglass's injunction to act goes a long way toward saving him from the power of his own words. He comments that "Like most other men, we had done the talking part of our work, long and well; and the time had come to *act* as if we were in earnest, and meant to be as true in action as in words" (*MBMF* 315). It also foreshadows his later decision to combine word and deed when he founds his own antislavery newspaper.

In describing Mr. Freedland's increased scrutiny of Douglass and the others of his group as they planned to escape, Douglass notes, as Du Bois later realized, that "Men seldom see themselves as others see them" (*MBMF* 308). At the time, Douglass believed that he and the others in his group were acting in a way that effectively concealed their true intentions of escape. It becomes clear to Douglass in hindsight that their intentions may have been conveyed through their buoyant singing of hymns emphasizing their goal of escape:

> "I thought I heard them say,
> There were lions in the way,
> I don't expect to stay
>   Much longer here.
> Run to Jesus—shun the danger—
> I don't expect to stay
>   Much longer here."
>
> (*MBMF* 308)

If Douglass played the double role of attempting to appear most satisfied at the time when he was most actively planning his escape, it is also clear that he also played doubled roles in other contexts of *My Bondage and My Freedom*. I have already noted in my discussion of the *Narrative* the ways in which Douglass comingles the sacred (which was itself doubled in the ways he plays Christian imagery against the folkloric imagery contained in Sandy Jenkins's superstitious "root") with the secular "religion" embodied in his earliest descriptions of the abolitionist movement.

II

The religiously charged death and resurrection described in the episode with Edward Covey gives way to the unsuccessful escape attempt that takes place during the Easter holiday. Douglass stands outside the circle of activity he describes, ultimately standing beyond the influence of either organized religion (Christian or otherwise) or the tightly circumscribed role proscribed him by his abolitionist supporters. As before, *My Bondage and My Freedom* suggests, for instance, that Douglass's interest in organizing a Sabbath school has virtually nothing to do with any kind of religiously inspired ministerial impulse. Instead, the Bible is merely the tool that allows him to achieve his goal, which is to teach other slaves to read. And if his growth can be charted as a series of ever-expanding concentric circles, then his eventual awareness of the limitations imposed by the abolitionists indicates that the movement itself became the tool that Douglass used to achieve the position as publisher of the antislavery newspaper the *North Star*. Through the apparatus of his own newspaper, he achieved the position of "representative man" that the earlier two narratives had been building toward and preparing him to assume.

Douglass's attraction to the ideals proposed by Garrison in *The Liberator* raises the abolitionist cause to the stature of revealed religion by referring to the ways "it preached human brotherhood, denounced oppression, and, with all the solemnity of God's word, demanded the complete emancipation" (*MBMF* 362) of African-American slaves. Garrison himself is described by Douglass (who refers to himself as a self-confessed "hero worshiper" by nature) as having a "heavenly countenance" for whom "The bible was his text book—held sacred, as the word of the Eternal Father—sinless perfection—complete submission to insults and injuries—literal obedience to the injunction, if smitten on one side to turn the other also" (*MBMF* 362). Garrison's appropriation of the biblical word foreshadows Douglass's subsequent appropriation. At this point, Douglass is content merely to listen and conceal his true thoughts behind a veil of acceptance: "It was enough for me to listen—to receive and applaud the great words of others, and only whisper in private, among the white laborers on the wharves, and elsewhere the truths which burned in my breast" (*MBMF* 363). Beyond simply being an emotional reaction to Garrisonian abolitionism, Douglass's formulation shows the authorizing mechanism through which his thoughts proceeded.

Immediately following this passage, Douglass discusses the Nantucket antislavery convention with which he concludes the *Narrative*. However, in the revised account, he reworks his thoughts about his initial speech and focuses as much on Garrison's speech as he does on his own halting, though apparently inspiring, speech. The account of his speech in the *Narrative* finds Douglass saying that "I spoke but a few moments, when I felt a degree of freedom, and said what I desired with considerable ease" (*N* 96). *My Bondage and My Freedom* finds Douglass considerably more uncertain and ill at ease with his "performance," writing that "it was with the utmost difficulty that I could stand erect, or that I could command and articulate two words without hesitation and stammering. I trembled in every limb" (*MBMF* 364). Why the apparent contradiction? Partially, the shift represents a difference in the rhetorical objectives of the two texts. The first text focuses on Douglass culturally authorizing himself by writing and speaking his cultural presence. The second text implicitly questions the mere acquisition of language and "voice." Instead, it seeks to assert the interpretive element that is the true basis of authority.[10]

His reaction to what Garrison says seems to look toward what he himself hopes rhetorically to accomplish: "[H]e possessed that almost fabulous inspiration, often referred to but seldom attained, in which a public meeting is transformed, as it were, into a single individuality—the orator wielding a thousand heads and hearts at once, and by the simple majesty of his all controlling thought, converting his hearers into the express image of his own soul" (*MBMF* 365). The power of the word implies to Douglass the possibility of transforming disparate entities into a single identity that reconciles the contradictions (slave and free, black and white, object and subject) that have characterized his life. There is a pattern of recreation that has redefined Douglass from slave to freeman in the earlier *Narrative* and that now focuses on Douglass's transformation from freeman to public figure. That recreation hinges on his realization that while the acquisition of literacy and the ability to manipulate language is important, the true power of language is held by the person authorized to interpret those words. Thus, Douglass's comment that after his speech Garrison took him "as his text" foreshadows Douglass's own attempts to textually reclaim himself. Douglass's involvement within the confines of the antislavery agenda suggests that the success of his recreation of himself is a function of his understanding of and ability to manipulate the "warring ideals" that informs Du Bois's racial and cultural formulation.

The moment in which he briefly forgot the meaning of race in the context in which he lived ("For a time I was made to forget that my skin was dark and my hair crisped" [*MBMF* 366]) was immediately reversed by the context in which his story was placed. After all, he was "generally introduced as a '*chattel*—a '*thing*'—a piece of southern '*property*' the chairman assuring the audience that *it* could speak" (*MBMF* 366). The danger of defining himself in terms of this kind of doubled identity became clear to Douglass as his work as a platform speaker continued. He was increasingly inclined to elaborate on his experiences as a slave while simultaneously being required by both his audience and his abolitionist sponsors to "Let us have the facts" (*MBMF* 367). Bakhtin writes that "[N]o living word relates to its object in a *singular* way: between the word and its object, between the word and the speaking subject, there exists an elastic environment of other, alien words about the same object, the same theme, and this is an environment that it is often difficult to penetrate. It is precisely in the process of living interaction with this specific environment that the word may be individualized and given stylistic shape."[11]

What the reader sees here are Douglass's attempts to negotiate an "elastic environment" in which he is simultaneously the author of his narrative and its subject. He is, as well, a freeman whose only option is to define himself in terms of being a slave.[12] The conflict to these doubled identities comes from both within and without. Douglass himself wanted to extend beyond the rigid limitations of his assigned role ("I was growing, and needed room" [*MBMF* 367]) and "felt like *denouncing*" (*MBMF* 367) the injustices he saw rather than simply narrating them. But that interior manifestation of identity, represented by his desire to explicate that which he spoke, is as fractured and disrupted as the external gaze directed at him by his audience and abolitionist sponsors. Both required a pattern of rhetorical behavior that was not fully reflective of his experiences. "People won't believe you ever was a slave, Frederick, if you keep on this way. . . . Be yourself . . . and tell your story. . . . Better have a *little* of the plantation manner of speech than not; 'tis not best that you seem too learned" (*MBMF* 367). The irony is that in contradicting many of the stereotypes his audience held concerning how former slaves should speak and tell their stories, Douglass uses the written word to convey the "facts" of his experiences. He therefore essentially becomes the subject of his own objectified, authorial gaze.[13]

Facts. Unvarnished, verifiable truth. These continued to be the keywords of the successful ex-slave narrator. At the conclusion of his narrative entitled *Narratives of the Sufferings of Lewis and Milton Clarke* (1846), for instance, Lewis Clarke even went so far as to include some of the questions he was most regularly asked in public interrogations following the oral rendering of his narrative: How do slaves spend the Sabbath? What do slaves know about the Bible? How is it that masters kill their slaves, when they are worth so much money? What do they do with old slaves, who are past labor?[14] This suggests that it was the oral component of their stories that served for the slave narrator to allay thoughts of fraud and inauthenticity in the minds of his or her audience. Douglass, though, chose to "dispel all doubt, at no distant day [the writing of the *Narrative*], by such a revelation of facts as could not be made by any other than a genuine fugitive" (*MBMF* 368). The oppositional pattern of the narrative encourages the reader to see Douglass's southern experiences as merely different in kind from his northern experiences. It seems equally useful to bear in mind that Douglass's rhetorical methods and objectives accordingly shifted to accommodate his expanding thoughts on race and American culture.[15] What had, in the *Narrative*, been an objective intent painstakingly to use biblical image and reference to authorize his individual position as a "genuine fugitive" had been transformed into the goal of establishing and expanding his position in a larger cultural space.

The question of authenticity or, for lack of a better word, "truth" has never been far removed from the slave narrator. At the core of this demand for "truth" has been an obligation to present some kind of verifiable referentiality. This was usually satisfied by the physical presentation of the former slave. The physical verified the rhetorical. Rarely, as in Douglass's case, was it the other way around. As I will explore at greater length in my discussion of *Incidents in the Life of a Slave Girl*, Harriet Jacobs faced this kind of scrutiny from the first appearance of her narrative because of critics who were unconvinced of where her authority ended and her editor's, Lydia Maria Child, began. Part of the danger Douglass encountered in essentially commodifying himself as the subject of his writerly "voice" was that his ability to extend himself beyond the constraints of the rubric in which he was forced to write and the ways in which he was able to construct himself ultimately fell short of Douglass's vision of himself.[16] Douglass, later in his long career, became increasingly concerned with the mythic qualities of his status as one of America's "Self-Made Men," a title he chose for a speech he regularly presented. That sense of being self-made (and self-revised) serves as the final structuring device in *My Bondage and My Freedom*. That sense of self-fabrication began with the fight with Covey that was the centerpiece of the *Narrative*, progresses to the sense of confinement he began to feel in his role as a platform speaker for the abolitionist cause, and concludes with his decision upon returning from England to begin his own newspaper.[17]

The manifestation of Douglass's "voice" does not find its greatest freedom in either of the first two narratives, but from the *North Star* whose title, appropriately, was subsequently changed to *Frederick Douglass' Weekly*. This was a platform that Douglass himself both created and sustained. *My Bondage and My Freedom* culminates with Douglass's description of overcoming the obstacles he encountered in achieving that goal. "I have now given the reader an imperfect sketch of nine years' experience in freedom," Douglass writes, "—three years as a common laborer on the wharves of New Bedford, four years as a lecturer in New England, and two years of semi-exile in Great Britain and Ireland. A single ray of light remains to be flung upon my life during the last eight years, and my story will be done" (*MBMF* 389). The strength of the opposition by Garrison and his followers comes from the unlikely source of those who initially encouraged Douglass. It parallels in narrative importance the opposition he received from Edward Covey.

But at this point, Douglass abandons the religious framework within which he has cast his earlier activities including the "death" he experiences on Friday afternoon, his "rebirth" on Sunday morning, his fight against the satanically rendered Edward Covey, Sandy's prophetic dreams, and the Judas-like kiss of whoever revealed the Easter plot of the group. Here, Douglass turns entirely to a morally defined secular rendering of his story. His earlier presentations of himself ultimately depict him as being a ghost in the abolitionist machine whose story is a fluid representation of experience designed to further the abolitionist cause. Douglass's "imperfect sketch" now reveals another part of the power of Douglass's ability to recreate his identity. His initial creation and subsequent revisions indicate both his concern with identity and his awareness of the culturally fabricated nature of African-American identity. Douglass's decision to begin a newspaper served as his own, self-constructed platform for his ideas and allowed him the freedom to present those ideas without the confinements of the slave narrative genre: "I already saw myself wielding my pen, as well as my voice, in the great work of renovating the public mind, and building up a public sentiment which should, at least, send slavery and oppression to the grave, and restore to 'liberty and the pursuit of happiness' the people with whom I had suffered, both as a slave and as a freeman" (*MBMF* 389).

Paradoxically, Douglass seeks to use his "voice" to detach himself from the very platform that initially gave him his "voice." He returns us to the question of "voice" and its relation to an African-American "voice" that is socially and rhetorically constructed. Douglass's earliest editorials in the *North Star* echoed the Garrisonian platform: The Constitution was a pro-slavery document, the American Union should be dissolved, the ballot was not an effective tool against slavery, and moral suasion was the primary force for abolitionists to use in bringing about the end of slavery. Douglass's conflict with the New England antislavery platform began in the spring of 1851 and subseqently grew in intensity to the point where his split with Garrison soon became complete. In *The Liberator* of January 18, 1856, Garrison called *My Bondage and My Freedom* "a remarkable volume, it is true, for its thrilling sketches of a slave's life and experience, and for the ability displayed in its pages, but which, in its second portion, is reeking with the virus of personal malignity towards Wendall Phillips, myself, and the old organizationists generally, and full of ingratitude and baseness towards as true and disinterested friends as any man ever yet had upon earth."[18]

The harshness of Garrison's angry response to Douglass's opinions is especially enlightening when read in relation to Douglass's restrained, intellectual recitation of what was clearly a bitter dispute:

> About four years ago, upon a reconsideration of the whole subject, I became convinced that there was no necessity for dissolving the "union between the northern and southern states;" that to seek this dissolution was no part of my duty as an abolitionist; that to abstain from voting, was to refuse to exercise a legitimate and powerful means for abolishing slavery; and that the constitution of the United States not only contained no guarantees in favor of slavery, but, on the contrary, it is, in its letter and spirit, an anti-slavery instrument, demanding the abolition of slavery as a condition of its own existence, as the supreme law of the land. . . . I mean, however, not to argue, but simply to state my views (*MBMF* 391–92, 393).

There are several fictions of self-creation at work here. First, there is the double act of self-creation, a component of all fugitive slave narratives, represented both in the act of escape as a creation of the self outside of slavery and in the decision of the narrator to write the story of his or her escape. Douglass was now free from slavery (though not necessarily from the effects of slavery or other forms of racism) and free rhetorically to recreate the events of his life. The concentrically circular form of *My Bondage and My Freedom* means that Douglass is doing all of this in addition to creating himself out of the encircling boundaries of the Garrisonian abolitionism that gave him a platform for the expression of his "voice." Through the agency of Garrisonian abolitionism, Douglass initially finds the language to critique slavery and America and subsequently realizes the limitations of the very institution that first gave him that platform. Ironically, in the same way former slaves took language and transformed it into something slaveholders never intended, so, too, does Douglass take the language of Garrisonian abolitionism and transform it into something abolitionists never intended.

In so many ways, *My Bondage and My Freedom* is a Janus-faced text that looks backward toward Nat Turner's millinarian impulses. It transfers the sacred element inscribed in Turner's text to the secular world, as well as to the problems of authentication and authority that Harriet Jacobs encountered in generations of responses to her narrative.

III

Douglass's double act of self-creation is intensified in Jacobs's *Incidents*. Her narrative was forced, both in the context and the particulars of its composition, to contend with the relative lack of opportunities for black women to write their stories and the difficulties inscribed in that lack of opportunity. The general context from which Jacobs's experiences and writings emerged meant that she had to contend with interlocking race, gender, and class issues. There were the obvious issues of African Americans as a group achieving their rights. But there was a concern among black women activists that the kind of roles related to American women as a whole would simply be applied to them. They were right. Even an ardent supporter of human rights like Frederick Douglass managed to make a profound distinction between the roles of black women and black men when he wrote in the August 24, 1849, edition of the *North Star* that "There is certainly something in the ordinance of human affairs, in the organization of society, which demands from the female sex the highest tone of purity and strictest observance of duties pertaining to woman's sphere."[19] Being relegated to that sphere meant that the participation of black women in the public arena created tensions between black women and their audiences (black and white) and between women and those blacks (male and female) who did not share their thoughts on the public and political engagement of African-American women.[20] They were strongly encouraged to adopt the attributes of piety, purity, domesticity, and submissiveness that characterized the nineteenth-century ideal of "true womanhood."[21]

The locus of "true womanhood" is very much the domestic sphere. Jacobs's decision to structure *Incidents* in terms of her ongoing quest to establish and maintain a home for herself and her children is an important statement concerning the various boundaries she is culturally required to assume in her narrative.[22] To a large extent, the issue of autonomy that Frederick Douglass encountered and that caused his final break with Garrisonian abolitionism was similar to the issues of autonomy that black women faced. The trend in African-American abolitionism in the 1830s and 1840s was toward increased independence for blacks and away from an overreliance on white antislavery organizations. As Douglass realized, there were limitations to what could be expected when various factions brought their strategies and concerns to the antislavery issue. These limitations also had a gendered component. Black women, who had initially formed antislavery societies like the Female Anti-Slavery Society of Salem in the early 1830s, found that when their society became racially integrated in 1834, their objective of black self-reliance became secondary to their endorsement of Garrisonian abolitionism.[23]

Implicit in the antislavery agenda was the understanding that although the system of slavery was inherently wrong, this did not imply a belief in either racial or gender equality. Indeed, there were strong distinctions made between support of the abolitionist agenda and concerns about racial miscegenation in the abolitionist press. A contributor to *The Liberator* commented that "Slavery is an evil of a great magnitude. . . . We do not believe it was the design of the Creator, that marriages should take place between negroes and whites, and certain we are, that such alliances will never be tolerated in New England."[24] Given the strong possibility that her narrative would find a hostile reaction from a number of fronts, how was Jacobs to frame and authorize her story in a way that made it her own, yet simultaneously made it a testimony of experience to which her audience could relate?

Douglass in *My Bondage and My Freedom* insists on taking his discursive product as his own by deciding to found the *North Star* and metaphorically creating his own platform for his thoughts. Jacobs is simultaneously more and less direct in her approach to the vexing issue of separating narrative "voice" from narrative subject. The most obvious act of separation comes from her decision to adopt the pseudonym of "Linda Brent" as a way of obscuring her relationship to the experiences described. That blurring of "fact" and "fiction" is preserved in rhetorical strategies throughout the narrative, including the admission in her Preface to the narrative that she had "concealed the names of places, and given persons fictitious names."[25] But paradoxically, perhaps, she concludes the Preface by saying "I want to add my testimony to that of abler pens to convince the people of the Free States what Slavery really is" (*I* 1–2). For Jacobs, the "real" is best described by that which is apparently "unreal." And in this case, descriptions of the "self" have much less to do with Jacobs as an individual self as they have to do with all the slave girls who have had similar experiences without the opportunity to write those experiences.

The environment of the narrative is as fractured as its reader: Harriet Jacobs has written a narrative of her own life using a pseudonymous narrator whom she calls Linda Brent. Linda Brent directs her story to a white, northern, female audience who may or may not be different from the actual readers of the book. The narrative strategy involved in fragmenting the apparent audience allows Jacobs to distance her reader from the audience to whom the text is narrated. Simultaneously, she draws the actual reader of the narrative into a position in which he or she is encouraged to sympathize with the implied audience while maintaining an awareness of its distance. This engaged distance mirrors the engaged distance Jacobs has rhetorically constructed for herself as the experiencer/writer of the events of the narrative and as the protagonist of the text.[26]

These rhetorical modes raise fundamental questions about the very elements of fictional self-creation upon which this study rests: What methods are available to slave narrative writers as authorizing techniques? And what happens if the fictionalizing aspects of their self-creation produce a text that paradoxically subverts the accepted techniques of representing "truth" even as it purports to tell that "plain truth"? This has been a concern of many of the scholars who have approached *Incidents*. Jean Fagan Yellin's authoritative text is as much a presentation of the narrative itself as it is a gathering of correspondence, notes, and illustrations intended to support a reading of the text that rescues it from simply being read as a "false slave narrative."[27] For some, it was perceived as being too representative of the collective experience of African-American slave girls comfortably to be seen as representing any individual identity whatsoever. This, after all, is the implicit basis of John Blassingame's influential judgment that "In spite of Lydia Maria Child's insistence that she had only revised the manuscript of Harriet Jacobs's [story] 'mainly for purposes of condensation and orderly arrangement,' the work is not credible."[28]

By emphasizing the issue of credibility, though, Blassingame is also reacting to the fact that Jacobs selectively increases and decreases the space between Linda Brent and the narratee (and by extension the actual reader). These literary techniques come perilously close to the modes characteristic of the sentimental fiction upon which the form of her narrative was based. Jacobs writes a text representative of all slave girls for a narratee representative of all white, northern, middle-class women, yet read by a reader who may or may not have shared those characteristics. As such, Jacobs works within a rhetorical space that is as boundaried and mediated as Turner's *Confessions*. *Incidents* is as strongly mediated by the narratee as Turner's text is mediated by

Thomas R. Gray. But the important distinction is that narrators like Douglass and Turner largely sought to distinguish themselves as much from their perceived reading audiences as they did from other slaves. Turner transforms himself into a prophetic figure ordained by God to carry out God's vision of a New Jerusalem. Frederick Douglass reconstructs himself into a figure representative of African-American possibility who is somehow in the circle though not necessarily of the circle of African-American experience, yet who is also unfit fully to accept or be accepted by those who initially offer him freedom. Both Turner and Douglass discursively authorize themselves by appropriating the power of religious rhetoric. They seek to particularize their experiences within the universalizing context of American slavery.

Conversely, Harriet Jacobs seeks to universalize her experiences in the context of a system of slavery that she sees as being remarkably particularizing.[29] The antislave system that encouraged male writers to produce their narratives was too narrow in its focus, however, to satisfactorily offer Jacobs the same opportunity. Jacobs herself was keenly aware of the disparity. In a letter to her friend Amy Post, Jacobs wrote, "I had determined to let others think as they pleased but my lips should be sealed and no one had a right to question me for this reason when I first came North I avoided the Antislavery people as much as possible because I felt that I could not be honest and tell the whole truth."[30] Ironically, the very values of truth and autonomous control over her own story that were so important to Jacobs were the very qualities upon which she was most strongly attacked by critics. The truth to which Jacobs aspires is very different from the kind of objective, factually derived truth that the antislavery agenda encouraged. For Jacobs, the "whole truth" (and the authorization of that truth) was a function of her ability to authorize herself within the self-referential context of her own words.[31]

In "*Doers of the Word*," Carla Peterson argues for a view of African-American women that sees them engaged in an attempt to transcend the limitations of the domestic sphere and enter the public arena. For many women, Peterson argues, the movement from politicizing the private into the public involved the engagement of religious evangelical language and imagery as a way of establishing for themselves a platform for their thoughts that the antislavery movement often denied them.[32] The question of how best to reconcile the role of women within the constraints of the abolitionist agenda became a formidable issue that ultimately contributed to divisions of the Massachusetts

Anti-Slavery Society and the American Anti-Slavery Society in 1839 and 1840, respectively. By using evangelical Protestantism to create a public presence for themselves, Carla Peterson argues that they created what she calls "hybrid spaces" for themselves.[33] The hybrid space that Jacobs creates is her text. That text engages elements of the slave narrative and sentimental novel literary genres while simultaneously refuting the strategies and expectations inscribed in both. Her rhetorically defined hybrid position allows her to incorporate in a single textual entity a series of oppositional elements. This permits her discursively to authorize the racial and gendered perimeter positions she is culturally forced to occupy.[34]

The prefatory material serves to illustrate some of the problems and possibilities the text creates for itself. In this instance, Jacobs takes the opportunity to frame her own text with her own words. She offers an explanation for why she has decided rhetorically to reconstruct the private experiences of her life into a representation of the collective experiences of black slave women ("But I do earnestly desire to arouse the women of the North to a realizing sense of the condition of two millions of women at the South, still in bondage, suffering what I suffered and most of them far worse" [*I* 1]). This explanation, along with the Introduction that follows, written by her editor, Lydia Maria Child, the opening chapters describing Linda Brent's childhood, and the body of correspondence outside the text between herself and the Quaker abolitionist Amy Post, also illustrates the sometimes unsettled associations that Jacobs established between herself and a series of white, female counselors in both the North and the South to aid her in her escape and in the eventual production of her narrative. That narrative is written in hopes of eliciting a sympathetic response from the women in the North to whom it is directed. The narrative also suggests in its direct addresses to the "reader," and in indirect assumptions, that the ideal reader of the narrative is somehow fundamentally unprepared fully to understand either the true significance of the narrative or the difficulties Jacobs faced in writing it. In her Preface, Jacobs even goes so far as to say that "Only by experience can any one realize how deep, and dark, and foul is that pit of abominations" (*I* 2).

The reason for the very existence of her narrative indicates that she deeply wishes to convey the essence of that "pit of abominations." There must be some reason for her construction of a narrative strategy that seeks to convey that which cannot be conveyed to those who are least prepared to receive it. Even the form of the narrative, which partially appropriates the conventions of both women's domestic fiction and the seduction novel, subverts Jacobs's ability adequately to discuss the subjects of sexuality and miscegenation that inform the narrative. Lydia Maria Child seems to recognize the difficulties contained in this problematic relationship of narrative arrangement. She writes in her Introduction that "I am well aware that many will accuse me of indecorum for presenting these pages to the public; for the experiences of this intelligent and much-injured woman [Brent] belong to a class which some call delicate subjects, and others indelicate. This peculiar phase of Slavery has generally been kept veiled; but the public ought to be made acquainted with its monstrous features, and I willingly take the responsibility for presenting them with the veil withdrawn" (*I* 4). The discomfort inscribed in Child's awareness of the discontinuities attached to the text reflects a larger discomfort with the perceived position of Jacobs's simultaneous role as subject and object.

Child also belies a curious discomfort with her dual role as supporter/collaborator for Jacobs and part of the sympathetic audience to whom the narrative is directed when she notes that "I do this for the sake of my sisters in bondage, who are suffering wrongs so foul, that our ears are too delicate to listen to them" (*I* 4). In attempting to identify with the experiences of her "sisters in bondage," Child maintains an awareness that that identification draws her and others like her ("our ears"), who are presumably sympathetic to those experiences, into a discomfortingly close personal relationship with a series of private experiences made public that may cause them to reconsider their assumptions about themselves. But in establishing this dynamic, Child threatens to transfer the locus of power away from the experiences Jacobs describes in the narrative itself and instead place its potential success or failure in the hands of its readers, who are called upon actively to exert their influence on behalf of other slave girls.[35] Southern control, institutionalized into slavery, has essentially been transferred to the North and institutionalized into the tenuous relationship of writer and audience.

Jacobs employs a number of traditions in telling her story. In so doing, she is able to see the compromised nature of her societal position. She stands beyond the ranks of slavery, for instance. But though indebted to prevailing attitudes of "true womanhood," she cannot fully claim that ideology as her own.[36] These thoughts, even beyond their relationship to what tools are used to put the story together (including the seduction novel, domestic fiction, and fugitive slave narrative), also speak toward the ways in which Jacobs authorizes her experiences. In "seeing" both the margins and the center, Jacobs is able to authorize her "voice" in the space between these extremes. In the prefatory material to the book, for instance, Jacobs's "voice" could profitably be read against the "voice" of Lydia Maria Child. This would serve as a way of arriving at some sense of where, in this narrative context, these arbitrarily assigned (and ever-shifting) boundaries stand in relation to each other. In seeking to give an explanation for the reasons why Jacobs was able to write so well, Lydia Maria Child offers a great deal of insight into the obstructions Jacobs faced: "[T]he mistress, with whom she lived till she was twelve years old, was a kind, considerate friend, who taught her to read and spell. Thirdly, she was placed in favorable circumstances after she came to the North; having frequent intercourse with intelligent persons, who felt a friendly interest in her welfare, and were disposed to give her opportunities for self-improvement" (*I* 3).

As Jean Fagan Yellin rightly notes in her Introduction to *Incidents*, a number of women in the South responded to Linda Brent's experiences as a woman and a mother over and above her experiences as a black woman and mother. But if, as she argues, white women in both the South and the North responded beyond the categories of race and class, how are we to read the implications of their actions (at least as Jacobs seems to see those implications)? Many of the women described in the narrative were willing to act in a responsible fashion as long as the boundaries of their "sisterhood" did not extend into the area of institutional influence. The mistress Brent describes in the opening chapter of the book, for instance, treated Linda's mother as "a slave merely in name" (*I* 7) and even taught Linda how to read and write. But upon her death, she bequeathed Linda in her will to her sister's five-year-old daughter. (The kind slaveholding mistress who eventually succumbs to the realities of the slave system is almost a stock character in the genre. Her appearance brings to mind Douglass's experiences with the kind Mrs. Auld.) The fact that this kind mistress is ultimately unable to transcend the institutionalized codes of conduct she encountered indicates much less about the strength of bonds between women and more about southern rules predicated on race and privilege.

This mistress's foil in the northern portion of Jacobs's story is Mrs. Bruce, to whom Jacobs reveals both her status as a runaway slave and the nature of her relationship with Mr. Sands. Though Mrs. Bruce's reaction is positive, the underlying dynamic between Jacobs's southern mistress and her northern mistress remains much the same. Jacobs is still forced to rely on Mrs. Bruce keeping her word within the circumscribed boundaries of cultural conduct. Her first mistress was ultimately unable to keep her word. Jacobs endows this with all the weight of New Testament significance: "My mistress had taught me the precepts of God's Word: 'Thou shalt love thy neighbor as thyself.' 'Whatsoever ye would that men should do unto you, do ye even unto them.' But I was her slave, and I suppose she did not recognize me as her neighbor" (*I* 8). The risk Jacobs faces in disclosing herself to Mrs. Bruce (much like the risk she faces in disclosing herself to her reader) is substantial.

Mrs. Bruce keeps the letter of her word to Jacobs. She, after all, does not return Jacobs to southern slavery. However, she violates the spirit of their agreement by offering to purchase Jacobs's freedom. Jacobs writes that "I felt grateful for the kindness that prompted this offer, but the idea was not so pleasant to me as might have been expected. The more my mind became enlightened, the more difficult it was for me to consider myself an article of property; and to pay money to those who had so grievously oppressed me seemed like taking from my sufferings the glory of triumph" (*I* 199). Mrs. Bruce has not purchased Linda for her services, and says as much. The very transaction itself, however, calls into question the actions of those women who work within the system on an individual basis. What I mean to suggest is that Mrs. Bruce had acted on Linda Brent's singular behalf without working toward a systematic change that would render these kinds of individual acts of genuine friendship, though friendships based on unequal levels of reliance and opportunity, unnecessary.

In addition to providing a northern foil to Brent's southern mistress, Mrs. Bruce serves the very important narratological function of standing in for the idealized "reader" to whom Jacobs writes and to whom she sometimes makes direct, editorializing comment. Mrs. Bruce, probably much like the "reader" from the author's Preface, whom Jacobs hopes to arouse to an awareness of the condition of slave girls, is also fundamentally unable fully to understand that experience. Yet even without fully understanding Linda's experiences, Mrs. Bruce has been able to bestow the relative freedom that none of those who understood the experience were able to do: "I remembered how my poor father had tried to buy me, when I was a small child, and how he had been disappointed. . . . I remembered how my good grandmother had laid up her earnings to purchase me in later years, and how often her plans had been frustrated. . . . My relatives had been foiled in all their efforts, but God had raised me up a friend among strangers, who had bestowed on me the precious, long-desired boon" (*I* 200–201). That "friend among strangers" is also the actual reader who also cannot fully identify with Brent's experiences and is less than likely to want to identify with a mode of response that is only partially adequate for effecting institutional rather than personal change. The difficulty the reader faces is in understanding that benevolent action like the action taken by Mrs. Bruce is appreciated at an individual level but does not go far enough truly to dismantle the institution.

The various asides to the reader by Jacobs emphasize an awareness that she has only been partially successful in conveying her true meaning. Taken in that light, she realizes that hers is a narrative of rhetorical and institutional failure. Whatever authority the narrative gains stems from its ability to establish itself and organize Jacobs's memory and experiences in the breech of discursive options available to it. Put differently, that space to which Jacobs aspires (that is, a space that can fully accommodate the realities of her sexual past and how those realities made it impossible for her to respond in ways that would be morally acceptable to her readers) simply does not exist. To a large extent, what Jacobs aspires to is an autonomy that takes her past into account while acknowledging the realities of her present.

That autonomy is encapsulated in her enduring vision of domestic peacefulness, which occupies the penultimate paragraph of the narrative: "The dream of my life is not yet realized. I do not sit with my children in a home of my own. I still long for a hearthstone of my own, however humble. I wish it for my children's sake far more than for my own" (*I* 201). This ongoing effort on Jacobs's part fully to realize her dream of a home reflects the narrative's pattern, which is a constant struggle against domestic dissolution. The narrative begins with Brent enjoying the warmth of a nuclear family in which her father is allowed to pursue work as a carpenter and "manage his own affairs" (*I* 5). But that warmth is eventually dissolved through the death of her mother and the reassertion of the realities of the slave system. Dr. Flint's home (and his offers to build a home for Linda in his efforts to seduce her) parodies the home in which Linda grew up and the home she continues to desire.

She briefly loses her home when she discloses her pregnancy to her grandmother in the chapter entitled "A Perilous Passage in the Slave Girl's Life," which has as much to do with her passage out of the encircling boundaries of domestic reassurance as it does with her passage out of the "innocent" days of her childhood. Her grandmother demands that she " 'Go away! . . . and never come to my house, again,' " to which Jacobs replies by writing "How I longed to throw myself at her feet, and tell her all the truth! But she had ordered me to go, and never to come there again. After a few minutes I mustered strength, and started to obey her. With what feelings did I now close that little gate, which I used to open with such an eager hand in my childhood! It closed upon me with a sound I never heard before" (*I* 57). The childhood Eden she describes in the first chapter has now been reduced to a memory. It soon dissolves into the attic of her grandmother's house. This crawlspace became her home for almost seven years where "The air was stifling; the darkness total. A bed had been spread on the floor. I could sleep quite comfortably on one side; but the slope was so sudden that I could not turn on the other without hitting the roof. The rats and mice ran over my bed" (*I* 114). The only thing making this existence bearable for her is her proximity to her children, though she largely cannot see them and cannot communicate with them.

Ultimately, the tone of dissatisfaction that concludes the narrative has to do with the fact that Jacobs has not been able fully to transcend the sense of obligation she feels to Mrs. Bruce: "But God so orders circumstances as to keep me with my friend Mrs. Bruce. Love, duty, gratitude, also bind me to her side. It is a privilege to serve her who pities my oppressed people, and who has bestowed the inestimable boon of freedom on me and my children" (*I* 201). The conditional nature of Jacobs's freedom coupled with her awareness of those conditions and her conditional acceptance of what that freedom means translates into some significant questions about the rhetorical authority of the narrative itself. Mrs. Bruce initially writes to Linda with the news that Dr. Flint is still searching for her with the intention of returning her to captivity in the South and that she intends to purchase Linda's freedom. Brent responds by writing to Mrs. Bruce with thanks "but saying that being sold from one owner to another seemed too much like slavery; that such a great obligation could not easily be cancelled; and that I preferred to go to my brother in California" (*I* 199). Given the imbalance of power inscribed in their relationship, it is obvious why Brent feels the weight of obligation.

Yet by extension, the narrative itself must also seek to reconcile the fact that Jacobs is very much dependent upon an autonomy that is essentially conferred upon her by her white supporters. She is unable to move beyond the rigid boundaries defined by her race even in the face of the kinds of appeals she has made to others who share her roles as women and mothers. Mrs. Bruce, a deep and cherished friend, is unable to see the ways in which her apparently benevolent actions bind the person whom she is attempting to liberate to an institutionalized system of oppression. How can Jacobs reasonably expect a reader, who is distanced from the experiences described in the narrative by the printed page itself, as well as by the various distancing features Jacobs has incorporated into the narrative, fully to understand what it is Brent intends to convey? And how, given the fact that the assumptions entitling southern control have been implicitly transferred to the North, can Jacobs hope to gain any level of control and authority over the rhetorical presentation of her own experiences?

IV

In the narrative, Jacobs places continuing emphasis on establishing a home for her children. This focus on home and motherhood connects her to the idealized reader she addresses throughout the text. Ultimately, though, these categories are of no use to Jacobs because hers is a narrative in which the politics of difference outweigh the politics of commonality. Brent does not achieve the home she so desires and her motherhood is tinged with the weight of moral violation and miscegenation.[37] If the success of the narrative, as Lydia Maria Child suggests in her Introduction, is a function of the response of the reader, it is not clear whether Jacobs has adequately constructed a case for authorizing her experiences. It is not even clear if she has the possibility of self-authorization in the narrow boundaries of these terms. Though she argues on her own behalf that "the condition of a slave confuses all principles of morality, and, in fact, renders the practice for them impossible" (*I* 55), that mode of authorization is dubious. It requires a revised understanding on the part of her readers not only of the slave girl's experiences but of their own reactions to those experiences within the context of their own lives. This process makes authorization an exterior rather than an interior event.

As outward-looking as the narrative is, however, its authorization ultimately comes from Jacobs herself and from her very act of writing. The responses to that act (and the relative notions of success or failure attached to those responses) are ultimately secondary to the power of the rhetorical act itself. Several weeks after Linda's arrival at the plantation, she witnesses Dr. Flint's beating of a male slave. According to the narrative, the exact cause of the beating is unclear. It is conjectured that the slave had either stolen corn or, in the presence of the overseer, had argued with his wife and "had accused his master of being the father of her child" (*I* 13). The slave and his wife continued to quarrel in the months following that beating and were eventually sold by Dr. Flint to a slave trader. This gave Dr. Flint "the satisfaction of knowing that they were out of sight and hearing. When the mother was delivered into the trader's hands, she said, 'You *promised* to treat me well.' To which he replied, 'You have let your tongue run too far; damn you!' She had forgotten that it was a crime for a slave to tell who was the father of her child" (*I* 13). This slave mother "forgets" the criminal nature of questioning the actions of her master and of speaking about the injustices committed against her. Dr. Flint's attempts to restrict the woman from telling her own story (and the repercussions attached to letting her tongue "run too far") suggest the importance of the act of narrative control. Even the slave community was forced to speculate about the reasons for the beating of the man and the eventual sale of the couple. Silence places authority for the narrative in the hands of Dr. Flint; Jacobs's disclosure of the details reclaims the story as an indictment against the rhetorical boundary Dr. Flint hopes to construct and enforce.

Sandra Gunning argues that the silence imposed upon Linda by Dr. Flint on one side and by the "delicate ears" of her readers on the other places her in the position of endorsing and perpetuating the myths of southern male morality and northern female delicacy by assuming the burdens of shame and disgrace.[38] I might add that by rhetorically exposing the tactics of oppression used in the South (typified in the character of Dr. Flint) to her idealized "reader," she incriminates that reader in the oppression. She also manages to move beyond the domestic sphere conventionally assigned to women into a more extensive critique of black female coercion based on silence and rhetorical control.

The narrative is structured in terms of the domestic settings Brent experiences. Each of these domestic contexts provides paradoxical views of familial relationship. These contexts emphasize the traditional values of the home, like familial connection and moral instruction. They also suggest that not only do these possibilities not fully exist for black women, but that the domestic environment invokes patterns of domination and control particular to black women. The first passage of domestic recollection at the beginning of the narrative is punctuated by the deaths of Linda's mother and a kind mistress. In their kindness and ability to provide a happy domestic environment, these women owe a great deal to the idealized image of Jacobs's reader. Jacobs immediately subverts any easy identification on the part of her reader with her kind mistress by noting that although kind in life, in death her mistress perpetuated the system of domination and control by bequeathing Linda to her sister's five-year-old daughter. The household of Dr. and Mrs. Flint that Brent enters is characterized from the start as a place of mental and physical abuse and sexualized aggression. Mrs. Flint "had not strength to superintend her household affairs; but her nerves were so strong, that she could sit in her easy chair and see a woman whipped, till the blood trickled from every stroke of the lash" (*I* 12). Dr. Flint is equally cruel and vicious. When she turns fifteen and Dr. Flint begins "to whisper foul words" in her ear, it is Brent, not her reader, who draws the veil of modesty: "He tried his utmost to corrupt the pure principles my grandmother had instilled. He peopled my young mind with unclean images, such as only a vile monster could think of. I turned from him with disgust and hatred" (*I* 27).

Her turning away is not enough. The home, that place her readers equated with safety and order, came to represent all the possibilities of disorder and disfunction. Mrs. Flint became as involved in the repression as her husband when she demands complete silence ("Dr. Flint swore he would kill me, if I was not as silent as the grave" [*I* 28]) from Linda. Before detailing the extent of her mistress's jealousy, Brent makes another defense to her reader of her reasons for using her narrative to break the code of silence: "Reader, it is not to awaken sympathy for myself that I am telling you truthfully what I suffered in slavery. I do it to kindle a flame of compassion in your hearts for my sisters who are still in bondage, suffering as I once suffered" (*I* 29). She correctly recognizes that her grandmother's ability to create fear in Dr. Flint's heart had to do with the fact that "she was known and patronized by many people; and he did not wish to have his villainy made public" (*I* 29). Yet in making that villainy public, both to her reader and to Mrs. Flint, Brent takes the chance that the person hearing that story of villainy could side with the victimizer rather than the victim. To a large extent, the nineteenth-century conception of the Cult of True Womanhood required women to maintain their silence, just as Brent is required to maintain hers, in the face of their own oppression. It should therefore come as no surprise that Mrs. Flint sides with her husband and transfers the blame back onto Linda.

Mrs. Flint ultimately fails to realize that her own oppression differs only from Linda's in magnitude. Why should Linda's reader reach a different conclusion? After confiding her master's intentions to Mrs. Flint, Linda realizes that Mrs. Flint "felt that her marriage vows were desecrated, her dignity insulted; but she had no compassion for the poor victim of her husband's perfidy. She pitied herself as a martyr; but she was incapable of feeling for the condition of shame and misery in which her unfortunate, helpless slave was placed" (*I* 33). Linda's testimony was ultimately unpersuasive to Mrs. Flint, who instead turned her attention to scrutinizing Linda rather than Dr. Flint. The shadow of Mrs. Flint's scrutiny that falls over Linda as she sleeps becomes as disconcertingly consuming as the shadow of Dr. Flint that falls over Linda as she kneels at her mother's grave. Linda's position as textual authority ("She now tried the trick of accusing my master of crime, in my presence, and gave my name as the author of the accusation" [*I* 34]) is ultimately undermined by a simple denial on Dr. Flint's part. Dr. Flint's rejection of Linda's testimony speaks toward the reality of Linda's position both as a slave girl and as an emancipated writer composing her own text: "I understood his object in making this false representation. It was to show me that I gained nothing by seeking the protection of my mistress; that power was still all in his own hands" (*I* 34).

Brent's narrative suggests more than an implicit correlation between her reader and Mrs. Flint. It suggests the implicit powerlessness of her position as former slave narrator seeking to represent both the injustices of the slave system and the conditions of acceptance that perpetuate it. Put differently, the continuation of oppression that Brent documents has relatively little to do with whether or not people have heard the truth but much more to do with the balance of power that skews the willingness of those who have heard the truth to act on that knowledge. My point here is that the limitations imposed upon the text from both within and without are fundamentally issues of rhetorical authority. And in relation to that authority, southern women give their interpretive responsibilities over to their husbands as completely as northern women give their interpretive responsibilities over to the state.

Brent's decision immediately to follow the description of her mistress's domestic activities with a passage indicting the Fugitive Slave Law indicates the way she sees the domestic sphere as having larger, public ramifications. In the South, the home encourages collusion between white women and the punishment meted out by their husbands. Corruption of women in the North occurs when they accept, by their inaction, oppressive legislation. The Fugitive Slave Law essentially erases the distinction between the North and the South by turning the North into "bloodhounds" for the South. Brent shows her unwillingness to submit to the platitudes Dr. Flint proposes when he says, "Poor, foolish girl! you don't know what is for your own good. I would cherish you. I would make a lady of you. Now go, and think of all I have promised you" (*I* 35). Yet when Linda thinks of it, she thinks of the way northern families fully accept the "imaginary pictures of southern homes. [T]hey are not only willing, but proud, to give their daughters in marriage to slaveholders. The poor girls have romantic notions of a sunny clime, and of the flowering vines that all year round shade a happy home. To what disappointments are they destined!" (*I* 35–36).

By taking action against the emptiness of this model, Brent accepts a domestic solution that further emphasizes the limitations, suggested here by physical encapsulation, of the home. In the chapter entitled "The Loophole of Retreat," Brent describes how she hides in the nine-by-seven attic space, which allows her to hear (and eventually see) her children below on the street. Brent is concerned about her children, yet the expression of her maternal role requires physical withdrawal. Here, as in previous domestic settings, Brent displaces her own rhetorical centrality by forcing her readers into a position in which they must see the precarious relationship between her sexual decisions and the politicization of her maternal role. Because of her strategy of emphasizing the commonalities of maternal concern with the realities of domestic oppression, Brent asserts her rhetorical control over her readers by asking them to understand what they do not and cannot know (the experience of slavery) in the context of that which they do know (motherhood).

According to Brent, her white audience was unequipped fully to understand the basis (and desperation) of her actions with Mr. Sands. Even her grandmother initially misunderstands the extent of her desperation. Brent's difficulties as a slave girl who acts against the oppression of the household is contrasted with her great-aunt Nancy. Aunt Nancy witnessed Linda's pursuit by Dr. Flint even as Aunt Nancy herself was being killed by her own sense of duty to Dr. and Mrs. Flint's household. Aunt Nancy's brief appearance in the narrative serves to highlight the possibilities of Brent's truly ideal reader. Aunt Nancy is both understanding and encouraging and, as the twin sister of Linda's mother, she doubles as a mother figure for Linda. Though confined to the Flint household, Aunt Nancy realizes that Linda's motherhood and continuing search for a home requires active involvement on Linda's part.

More importantly, Aunt Nancy understands the importance of words. Brent notes that "After I was shut up in my dark cell, she stole away, whenever she could, to bring me the news and say something cheerful. How often did I kneel down and listen to her words of consolation, whispered through a crack! . . . A word from her always strengthened me; and not me only. The whole family relied upon her judgment, and were guided by her advice" (*I* 144). In addition to being an ideal reader of Linda's experiences, Aunt Nancy is also, in her devotion to the Flints, the epitome of the devoted and loyal slave woman. She is idealized by the Flints to the point that Mrs. Flint wants her buried in Dr. Flint's family burial place. This causes Linda to speculate that possibly Mrs. Flint "thought it would be a beautiful illustration of the attachment existing between slaveholder and slave, if the body of her old worn-out servant was buried at her feet" (*I*146). For all of her verbal encouragement to Linda, Aunt Nancy loses the power of speech in her final days. With the emphasis she places on combining words and actions, she suggests Linda's simultaneous function as subject and object in the narrative. Like Linda, she places a priority on her responsibilities as a maternal figure; and as Linda realizes during her incarceration in her grandmother's attic crawlspace when her own health begins to falter, adherence in the South to that proscribed role is ultimately fatal to black women.

As I mentioned earlier, the final domestic sequence of the narrative, in which Linda reenters the Bruce family, is considerably more indicative of the possibilities of cooperation between blacks and whites and between women, though it is not without limitation and boundary for Linda. The fact that Linda notes that the second Mrs. Bruce was "brought up under aristocratic influences, and still living in the midst of them" (*I* 190) not only indicates a way of distinguishing a truer aristocracy with the pale facsimile of southern aristocracy she encountered as a member of the Flint household, but also emphasizes the continued commodification of Linda's experience. In the South, Linda was constrained by her status as property. Though the Bruces welcome Linda into their household and actively participate in her emancipation, she is still a runaway slave whose "freedom" is compromised by the very fact that she had to be "bought."

I do not mean to suggest that Mrs. Bruce has knowingly compromised Linda's freedom in any way. To the contrary, she has gone so far as metaphorically to place herself in Linda's position as a mother deprived of her child by offering to allow her own child to become a fugitive of the law and by placing herself in a position to be charged with violating the Fugitive Slave Law by harboring a slave wanted by her former master. The Bill of Sale stands as a written representation recording "the progress of civilization in the United States" (*I* 200). But the fact that it is a written representation, much like the written representation of Linda's narrative, gives it a value far beyond its intrinsic worth. Mrs. Bruce's hatred of slavery, her financial resources, and her eventual purchase of Linda's freedom link Mrs. Bruce as closely to an idealized version of what Brent's audience could accomplish if they were moved to activity as she is to the abolitionist women like Amy Post and Lydia Maria Child, who sponsor and support Jacobs in her attempts to write and publish her narrative. Similarly, women like Post and Child can be seen as having their own politicized agenda for encouraging a former slave woman to tell her story to northern white women, who themselves could be seen as being enslaved by their silence regarding the injustices of marriage and the home.

The Bill of Sale speaks beyond the gulf of silence that characterizes and defines slave experience. For Brent, the word, and especially the written word, contains a power to order, arrange, and transmit meaning to a continuous pattern that is in stark contrast to her constant struggles against the domestic annihilation she otherwise faces. Dr. Flint has earlier suggested and enforced the code of silence by whipping the slave woman who "let her tongue run too far" (*I* 13). There is a great deal to be said for the argument that the combined effects of the Fugitive Slave Law and the Dred Scott decision changed the structure of black autobiography by changing the texture of the narrative from a linear movement from slavery to freedom to a series of circular movements describing different kinds of boundaried experience.[39] The circularity depicted in *Incidents* brought with it increased camouflaging and masking. The narrative itself, with its use of pseudonyms and its unwillingness to see the North as substantially different from the South, creates a correlation to the letters Linda exchanges with Dr. Flint. These letters are intended to create a space for Linda by redirecting his attention away from her. The narrative gains its authority by using Linda's nearly seven-year attic stay to transform herself from possibly becoming an actual representation of the "madwoman in the attic." Instead, she uses her writing to claim power and authority for herself. This authority extends from the power she claims over Dr. Flint and into the production of the narrative itself.

In the chapter entitled "Competition in Cunning," Brent offers her readers an example of the ways in which black writing can be co-opted and misread by white readers. In this brief chapter, Linda decides from her hiding place in her grandmother's attic to match her cunning against Dr. Flint's continued desire to find her. She writes him a letter that she arranges to have postmarked from New York. Her hope is to convince Dr. Flint that she is no longer in the area and to give him false leads regarding her whereabouts. What is so disturbing about this passage is that in a narrative ostensibly based on the forthright, Linda has resorted to the duplicitous in order to gain the advantage. Her strategy in writing the letter to Dr. Flint is not far removed from her strategy in writing the narrative. Each suggests that as her rhetorical power grows, the way in which she depicted herself became increasingly veiled. Her letter to Dr. Flint separates subject and object (Brent as the writer of the letter vs. Brent as the object of Dr. Flint's sexual obsession) in much the same way the narrative separates Jacobs, the actual writer of the narrative from Linda, the body of her pseudonymous narrator.

But Brent's letters to Dr. Flint from the attic suggest a great deal more than simply presenting her in the tradition of the African-American trickster figure. Brent has written earlier in the narrative that one of Dr. Flint's strengths was the ability to convey his intentions, "manifested in signs" (*I* 31). Linda's appropriation of Dr. Flint's semiotic vocabulary suggests an appropriation of the authority associated with that vocabulary. By simultaneously sending letters to Dr. Flint and her grandmother, Brent gives her reader an opportunity to see that arriving at the "whole truth" requires seeing words in a larger context of meaning and interpretation. Clearly, many readers are unable fully to derive meaning from Brent's descriptions of her experiences. Mrs. Flint is clearly a less-than-ideal reader and, though "She watched her husband with unceasing vigilance" (*I* 31), was unable to determine his meaning. Even Brent's grandmother felt her plan to use the letters to manipulate Dr. Flint misguided. Of the women informed of the plan, only Linda's Aunt Nancy is encouraging. But after sending the letters and eagerly anticipating the satisfaction of throwing Dr. Flint off her track, Linda is shocked to hear during Dr. Flint's visit to her grandmother's house that "He had suppressed the letter I wrote to grandmother, and prepared a substitute of his own" (*I* 130).

The lesson Linda learns is similar to the lesson her narrative imparts to her reader, which is the importance of active interpretation of those experiences that otherwise appear to be completely transparent. To a greater extent, the cultural landscape that Brent attempts to describe is too fragmented to be fully understood by anyone who has not experienced slavery. The ultimate authority of the narrative, then, is much less a function of the reality she describes, the actual names of the those involved whom she suppresses, or even the actual name of the author herself. It has much more to do with the clues it provides for the ways in which a fragmented, often conflicting, cultural context needs to be examined and interpreted in order to be understood.[40] The territorial space the narrative seeks to establish for itself is conflicted, however, by the fact that while asking her reader to examine the submerged purposes inscribed in what appears to be the most clearly apparent of texts, the narrative concurrently implores the reader to be sympathetic to an alternative method of textual understanding. Furthermore, this revised method of understanding is being put forth within the already problematic paradigm of a former-slave author who, by her own account, has broken the moral codes assigned to her (though, as she explains, for the obvious reasons of fear and desperation) and her presumably white audience who is assumed to have no true context for understanding the "truth" of the slave experience anyway.

5

Ambiguity, Passing, and the Politics of Color: The Reconstruction of Race in William and Ellen Craft's *Running a Thousand Miles for Freedom*

I have said that the slave was a man.
—Frederick Douglass, *My Bondage and My Freedom*

I found that she made a most respectable looking gentleman.
—William Craft, *Running a Thousand Miles for Freedom*

THE NARRATIVES I examined in the preceding chapters were all linked by the fact that those who told the stories spent a great deal of time discussing the conditions of their slavery and the circumstances that led them to seek to escape. Several narrators devoted part of their story to addressing the relatively compromised nature of the freedom they eventually achieved. In each of those instances, however, the reason for the existence of the story had little to do with the particulars of the escape itself. The narratives had a great deal more to do with the fact that the narrator sought to displace the authority of those whose voices encircled their narrative and replace it with their own authorized versions of their history and experience.

In these respects, *Running a Thousand Miles for Freedom; or, the Escape of William and Ellen Craft from Slavery* (1860) is substantially different. *Running a Thousand Miles for Freedom* is, after a relatively brief exposition of the conditions of slavery, the account of a tense and thrilling escape. William and Ellen Craft, a married slave couple living in Georgia, realize that their best hope for a successful escape is for Ellen Craft, who has fair skin coloring, to pass as a white man accompanied to the North by her husband, who would masquerade as her trusted slave companion. In contrast, the *Narrative of the Life of Frederick Douglass* completely omits details concerning his escape. Instead, it focuses on an extensive analysis of the cultural conditions that defined Douglass as a slave and encouraged his desire to extend beyond those confines. Whereas other slave narrators address the issue of authenticity and identity by rhetorically usurping and redefining the written expression of their experiences, the Crafts use their escape to address these issues by calling into question the very basis of traditional classifications of race, class, gender, and the master/slave relationship.[1]

Their mode of cultural authorization is substantially different from Frederick Douglass, Harriet Jacobs, or even Nat Turner (by way of Thomas R. Gray). They engineer their escape on the belief that the masks they assume are not fixed and unchanging, although culturally stereotyped responses to those masks may be relatively fixed. Essentialist views of either race, class, or gender mistakenly consider these as discrete categories, thus ignoring the fact that assumptions about any one aspect within one of these categories necessarily shapes assumptions and responses to any other aspect of that category. Ellen Craft, for instance, cannot pass for white without some assumptions about blackness. Neither can she pass for a master without an articulation of what it is to be a slave.[2]

W.E.B. Du Bois's thoughts on the veil (and its configuration of alternate experiences in front of and behind the veil) suggests Ralph Ellison's modification of those ideas in his thoughts on visibility and invisibility.[3] Each of these formulations relies on visual recognition and emphasizes a binary component. While the emphasis on vision as a primary component of understanding is useful, the starkly binary context of these thoughts obscures, as *Running a Thousand Miles for Freedom* suggests, the fact that there are many systems of understandability. The act of passing involves much more than simply one who passes and one who is gulled. Passing threatens to subvert the markers and identifiers inscribed in a system in which racial identity delimited social position and possibility. Passing also calls the very definition of identity into question. Because someone was able to transcend the lines of demarcation enclosing race and gender, the qualities contained within those designations can no longer comfortably be regarded as constant and immutable. The metaphor of race and gender now suggests something remarkably incorporeal that can somehow be conquered by a series of visual understandings based on various appropriations of racialized, gendered qualities.

In terms of race and racial subordination, then, whiteness brought with it not only obvious social privileges. It also, and more importantly in many ways, brought with it the privilege of not being classified or defined at all. Whiteness served as a racial and cultural point of origin against which all others were evaluated and determined. The performative aspects of race (either blackness or whiteness) offer a way of reinterpreting racial designation as a mask worn by whites as well as blacks that marks all who are touched by it. In *Running a Thousand Miles for Freedom*, the narrative's focus is subtly shifted away from an exposition of what it is to be black in the United States toward an examination of the meaning of whiteness.[4]

I

Whereas the stories of many other fugitive slaves relied on the strategy of situating white readers in a position in which they had no other choice as clear-thinking, moral, Protestant Christians but to acknowledge the inherent immorality of the slave system, William and Ellen Craft placed these same readers in a position that relied less on their moral elevation and significantly more on taking from them the privileges their whiteness conferred upon them. Though whiteness assumed for itself a central position that was exempt from the scrutiny of racial description (or even the need to acknowledge those classifications), the Craft's narrative argues for a reading of race that sees whiteness as a socially constructed antithesis to blackness as well as a social fabrication that is as artificial as its arbitrary construction of blackness.[5]

The shift in perspective is subtle but important. Whiteness was no longer an objective yardstick of subjectivity. Whiteness itself became the object of scrutiny and inspection by a black subject intent on unmasking the fact that whiteness was as much a performance as it was a condition of existence. Thus, because Ellen Craft could successfully perform the role of a white man, the reader is left to contemplate the possibility that if whiteness is open to question and reevaluation, then by virtue of its culturally defined antithetical relationship, blackness is open to a similar reconsideration. After all, *Running a Thousand Miles for Freedom* has virtually nothing to do with offering Ellen Craft as an accurate representation of what it is to be white. Racial definition is not presented in a way that even remotely suggests that its interpretation is rooted or determinate. What William and Ellen Craft did as they formulated their escape plan was to rely on visually orienting their charade in terms of their understanding of their conception of white identity. They then used that view of white identity to translate her disguise into what others see when they see whiteness.

The sense of doubling oriented around the gaze and the act of seeing also involves the reader, who is placed in a position that momentarily allows access to both sides of the veil. This unique position serves to emphasize the distance between self-identity and the socially constructed version of that identity. The irony is that the social culture the Crafts encountered viewed passing as the dilemma and found a certain amount of assurance in the fact that passing of any form was impossible. The person attempting to pass would most certainly be recognized as attempting to be something he or she was not. In a much larger sense, though, what is at stake is not the transgression of passing. The true dilemma for those interested in maintaining absolute distinctions is the permeability of a way of knowing and apprehending identity that requires visual checks and balances to read and interpret the text of what is authentic or inauthentic.

The preface to the narrative notes, appropriately enough, that "This book is not intended as a full history of the life of my wife, nor of myself."[6] Indeed, it is "about" neither of their lives. It is "about" the performance they enact in which they subvert conventional understandings of traditional visual methods of classification concerning race, gender, and class. Thus, right from the start of the narrative, William Craft is able to address the theme of categorization undermined by the inability of visual reference to police its borders: "Notwithstanding my wife being of African extraction on her mother's side, she is almost white—in fact, she is so nearly so that the tyrannical old lady to whom she first belonged became so annoyed, at finding her frequently mistaken for a child of the family, that she gave her when eleven years of age to a daughter, as a wedding present" (*RTMF* 2). The black child, ostensibly white, who is able unwittingly to pass serves the dual purpose of critiquing the ways in which slave families were broken apart at the whim of self-indulgent slaveowners (a conventional element of fugitive slave narratives) and introducing the subversive element of passing upon which the narrative is based. The narrative itself becomes a kind of double-voiced instrument that finds different ways of speaking to different readers of the text. The narrative, for instance, finds a way to address issues of truth, verisimilitude, and cultural anxieties concerning the reality and maintenance of whiteness. The narrative also finds a way to cast William Craft, the narrating author, as an active participant in the rhetorical reproduction of whiteness and his wife Ellen as the objective reality of that cultural apprehension.

In constructing the narrative, William Craft deftly avoids addressing the issue of how identity is connected to language. Instead, he argues for an understanding of identity that sees it as a socially constructed artifact intended to differentiate between those embraced by social privilege and those excluded from it. As a social construction, identity is therefore circumscribed by the social constructions of the law. So, after telling the story of how his wife was frequently mistaken for a member of her slaveowner's family rather than a slave, William Craft turns his attention to the law itself and its unreliability as a way of policing the boundaries of race and privilege. But rather than initially presenting a description of the harsh realities of being black in this system, Craft turns to white people who are mistaken for black: "It may be remembered that slavery in America is not at all confined to persons of any particular complexion; there are a very large number of slaves as white as any one; but as the evidence of a slave is not admitted in court against a free white person, it is almost impossible for a white child, after having been kidnapped and sold into or reduced to slavery, in a part of the country where it is not known (as often is the case), ever to recover its freedom" (*RTMF* 2–3). Though he is unwilling or unable adequately to offer an historicized explanation of either himself or his wife, he *is* able to historicize the realities of slavery by emphasizing memory ("It may be remembered") and then calling into question the direction of the pass.

The *Oxford English Dictionary* offers a definition of passing that emphasizes the sense of movement, "progression or moving on from place to place," in its meaning. The generally accepted view of passing had to do with the anxiety on the part of those in the dominant culture of black people moving from the minority into the dominant culture. Craft suggests that that movement also involved the possibility of white people passing against their will into slave culture. Craft notes that "I have myself conversed with several slaves who told me that their parents were white and free; but that they were stolen away from them and sold quite young. As they could not tell their address, and also as the parents did not know what had become of their lost and dear little ones, of course all traces of each other were gone" (*RTMF* 3).

William Craft even adds to the anxiety of the free person being mistaken for a slave and taken into bondage by including the story of Salomé Muller. She was one of two daughters of German immigrants who arrived in New Orleans from Alsace in 1818. According to the story Craft recounts, their father took them to work on a plantation. He died soon thereafter. When surviving relatives sent for the two girls, all traces of their whereabouts had disappeared. One daughter was given up for dead. Nothing was heard of Salomé between 1818 and 1843, when Salomé was discovered by a woman who had emigrated to the United States with the Mullers. Salomé was immediately taken to the home of her cousin and godmother "who no sooner set eyes on her" before she was able positively to identify Salomé. Salomé's "identity was fully established" on the basis of the testimony of others who had seen her as a child. Even her birthmarks were entered as evidence of positive identification. Furthermore, "there was no trace of African descent in any feature of Salomé Muller" (*RTMF* 5). The case was elaborately argued in lower courts before the Supreme Court decided " 'she was free and white, and therefore unlawfully held in bondage' " (*RTMF* 6).

Lest William Craft's reader's fail to absorb the importance to the system of mistaken identity, he adds a story referenced in *Picture of Slavery* (1834) in which the Reverend George Bourne tells the story of how "a white boy who, at the age of seven, was stolen from his home in Ohio, tanned and stained in such a way that he could not be distinguished from a person of colour, and then sold as a slave in Virginia. . . . I have known worthless white people to sell their own free children into slavery; and, as there are good-for-nothing white as well as coloured persons everywhere, no one, perhaps, will wonder at such inhuman transactions" (*RTMF* 6–7). Not only is the young boy literally blackened, but his blackening comes at the hands of unscrupulous white people. The boy was not merely mistakenly identified as black. He was deliberately stolen and enslaved, thus mirroring the experiences of the black people who were intentionally stolen from Africa and enslaved in America. While mirroring the experiences of black slaves in America, this innocent young boy also mirrors the anxieties of those readers who themselves are incorporated into the narrative far beyond their own voyeuristic impulse simply to read the story of the thrilling escape of William and Ellen Craft from slavery.

There is a mechanism attached both to passing and to keeping people from passing. That mechanism allows the pass successfully to happen. Those who, for whatever reason, wish to keep others out of their social division rely on a visual recognition of that apparatus.[7] One would presumably recognize on the part of the person attempting to pass the elements of passing that would need to be employed and, on the basis of that knowledge, close ranks. Though *Running a Thousand Miles for Freedom* refutes that as an absolute safeguard, it suggests that if one were mistakenly to pass in the "other" direction (that is, from white to black), the legal restrictions intended to prevent blacks from infiltrating the ranks of whiteness would also deny whites the possibility of exiting the ranks of blackness. The narrative's audience could no longer enjoy the apparent comfort of an objective distance. By employing legal example, Craft's narrative voice subverts the infallibility of the gaze by initially asserting a variousness of blackness that the gaze fails fully to comprehend. For William Craft, there are no fully objective cross cultural points of reference. Therefore, any notions of identity are externally authorized by the stereotyped expectations of white readers of that identity. Rather than voyeuristically observing the actions of the black subjects contained in the narrative, white readers paradoxically find the concept of whiteness pulled forward for observation by the story's black narrator.

William Craft prefaces his description of the escape he and Ellen accomplished with several pages of laws regarding slavery: "I must now give the account of our escape; but, before doing so, it may be well to quote a few passages from the fundamental laws of slavery; in order to give some idea of the legal as well as the social tyranny from which we fled" (*RTMF* 13). Slavery and, by extension, its dependence on easily identifiable racial identity, argues for a view of race that emphasizes the truly arbitrary nature of racial identification and classification. The law itself becomes a fiction of self-creation by virtue of its very capriciousness. The distinctions involved in classifying black and white require a way of marking blackness as socially different. Ellen Craft's ability to pass, however, suggests that without some easily identifiable imprint of race, race itself turns into a socially inscribed marker in which the imprint has no true distinguishing content. I say all of this without overtly attempting to undermine the obvious reasoning of the narrative, which is that a black slave woman was able successfully to pass for a free white man with the social standing adequate enough to own a slave.[8]

Ellen Craft's ability to move between legal definitions and visual understandings of race does more than simply indicate that race is a social fabrication that can (for some, at least) be easily manipulated. By foregrounding the performative act of passing, the narrative suggests that passing is a viable strategy for a narrative subject to use in establishing an authorized identity. This sidesteps the ongoing discussion concerning whether or not race is somehow a social construction involving a series of shared values and assumptions or an essential aspect of being. But in the case the narrative presents, there is no transcendent truth because the basis of distinction, however applied, is completely arbitrary and open to question.[9]

For Ellen, there are the additional memories of what she has seen as a slave girl who was taken from her mother and who herself risks becoming a mother and having her child taken from her: "She had seen so many other children separated from their parents in this cruel manner, that the mere thought of her ever becoming the mother of a child, to linger out a miserable existence under the wretched system of American slavery, appeared to fill her very soul with horror; and as she had taken what I felt to be an important view of her condition, I did not, at first, press the marriage, but agreed to assist her in trying to devise some plan by which we might escape from our unhappy condition, and then be married" (*RTMF* 27). Ellen's view of the realities of her condition prompt her to accept the danger of passing as a white man in order to escape: "She saw that the laws under which we lived did not recognize her to be a woman, but a mere chattel, to be bought and sold, or otherwise dealt with as her owner might see fit. Therefore the more she contemplated her helpless condition, the more anxious she was to escape from it" (*RTMF* 30). The dual roles (slave and master, black woman and white man, property and property owner) that Ellen Craft is forced to occupy seem to force the reader into a position of paradoxical understanding. His or her social location is transformed into a function of the black gaze that could be manipulated and co-opted as necessary. The black gaze could no longer be assumed to be entirely passive and without volition and self-determination.

The reader is furthermore forced into a position in which he or she must recognize Ellen Craft as fulfilling an emblematic role in the escape portion of the narrative whose meaning cannot be fully confined or fixed. Ellen's passing gives William the opportunity to write a text asserting multiple conflicting interpretations. That text potentially reproduces for the reader the sense of instability Ellen's shifting identities suggest. The sense of instability inscribed in Ellen's role is played out both intratextually in the ways in which she is able to fool others and intertextually in the ways in which the rhetorical method of the narrative seeks to make the implied assurances between the reader and the text less secure. The direction of narrative account is completely transformed when a black woman chooses to imitate whiteness and maleness. She therefore makes the implied white reader reassess his or her sense of black female subordination.

The law, presented as a container inadequate for defining or maintaining the borders of racial distinction, turns into one of the ways the Crafts are able to execute their plan: "It is unlawful in Georgia for a white man to trade with slaves without the master's consent. But, notwithstanding this, many persons will sell a slave any article that he can get the money to buy. Not that they sympathize with the slave, but merely because his testimony is not admitted in court against a free white person" (*RTMF* 30). Yet, in offering the testimony of the narrative itself, William Craft does just that: He testifies against the apparent freedom of whiteness itself. At this point in the narrative, the issue of whiteness almost becomes secondary to the related issues of gender and class. Ellen realizes that as an illiterate slave, she would be unable to carry out the appropriate codes of conduct associated with the class into which she passed, namely, the ability to sign her own name in hotel registers. Neither would she be able to engage her fellow male travelers in the conversation expected of a gentleman.

II

In disrupting traditional understandings of the situations attached to race, the narrative also disrupts accepted procedures for presenting the slave experience. The narrative interrupts the traditional authority of experiential presentation and thereby reconfigures the elements of that mode of presentation. By changing the accepted frames of reference, the narrative also questions the validity of traditional experiential presentation. Since the text questions traditional frames of reference, the aligning purpose of those societal contexts is essentially

destroyed. With a number of notable exceptions, fugitive slave narrators were traditionally assumed to be men. Black women largely disap-
pear and seemingly become nonexistent on both sides of the veil.[10]
This reading seems especially applicable to the experience of Ellen
Craft, who simultaneously ceases to be black, a slave, a woman, or a
wife. She does not even function as the narrator of her own story. Yet
prior to the escape sequence, Ellen is remarkably active. Much of the
planning is hers. And during the escape, its success or failure rests
on her shoulders. If she either unconsciously missteps or consciously
chooses not to continue the ruse, their hopes for success vanish. But
during the escape itself, when she assumes the clothes, the poultice
(the handkerchief obscuring her face), the green spectacles veiling her
eyes, and the short-cropped haircut that constitutes her costume, she
becomes considerably more passive, relying fairly heavily on the costume to do what it was intended to do.

Even William admits that he "found that she made a most respectable looking gentleman" (*RTMF* 35), thus equating whiteness with
the gentleman class. Skin color clearly precludes the possibility that
one who is not white could ever hope to be considered a gentleman.
Indeed, William goes on to say that "There are a large number of free
negroes residing in the southern States; but in Georgia (and I believe
in all the slave States,) every coloured person's complexion is *prima
facie* evidence of his being a slave" (*RTMF* 36). Yet the sequence in
which Ellen appropriates the trappings of the southern gentleman, a
category whose membership is restricted to white men, she forces the
reader to reevaluate the apparent genetic predisposition of those qualities. The reader is implicitly encouraged to accept a realignment in
which the preferred qualities of the culture (humanity, judiciousness,
tenacity, and perseverance, among others) can be embodied in the
character of a black slave woman posing as a white southern gentle-
men. The symbolic message is clear: White Americans should not
blithely assume an intrinsic race-, gender-, or class-based separation,
especially if that separation is maintained only on the basis of some
easily fabricated realization of whiteness, maleness, or class. One de-
rives from the others and none can be adequately defined without
reconciling the presence of the others.[11]

During the escape portion of the narrative, Ellen displays a remarkable ability to challenge a series of raced, classed, and gendered associations. It almost seems as if this area of the text was intended momentarily to destabilize Ellen's identity in an effort to encourage the

reader to construct an interpretation of the narrative that emphasizes the plural nature of identity in general (as evidenced by Ellen's multiple masks and by the inability of social filters to maintain a sense of conformity). Readers of the text, mirrored by the readers within the text who fail to see Ellen for what she is, desire an essential rendering of race, gender, and class that Ellen's passing undermines.[12] Individual identity is eroded in direct relation to the societal world that so imperfectly contains that identity.

There is a deep, unrelenting anxiety about roles and identities within the text as well as without. Ellen, after all, is being required in the context of the escape ruse to accept a series of role reversals that place her in a position of power and authority over her own husband.[13] As they begin their escape by boarding a train north, William notes "I took the nearest possible way to the train, for fear I should be recognized by some one, and got into the negro car in which I knew I should have to ride; but my *master* (as I will now call my wife) took a longer way round, and only arrived there with the bulk of the passengers" (*RTMF* 42). For William, Ellen's passing is as much a transference of her role as his wife as it is a transference of her role as a black slave woman.

There is a narratological component at work in which William replaces the authority he has lost as Ellen's husband transformed into Ellen's slave with the authority he gains from serving as Ellen's "voice." A question remains concerning the way in which William is able to see and rhetorically construct Ellen's experiences during the escape, though. Because of laws prohibiting blacks and whites from traveling together, William and Ellen spend a large part of their time apart from one another. Ellen becomes a function of the gaze as much for William, the mediator of her narrative, as she is for the white passengers for whom she performs.

The difficulty the narrative faces in adequately representing Ellen is not limited to rhetorical representation. The narrative's frontispiece (see Illustration 5.1) also indicates an anxiety concerning how best to portray Ellen. During their final preparations for escape, William notes that "It then occurred to her that the smoothness of her face might betray her; so she decided to make another poultice, and put it in a white handkerchief to be worn under the chin, up the cheeks, and to tie over the head. This nearly hid the expression of the countenance, as well as the beardless chin" (*RTMF* 34–35). Yet that is not the view of Ellen visually represented in the engraving: "The poultice is left off in the engraving, because the likeness could not have been taken well with it on" (*RTMF* 35). What is unclear is whose likeness would be obscured by the poultice. Is the engraving intended to represent Ellen, William's wife? Or is the engraving intended to show Ellen in the disguise she used to pass as a white gentleman traveling with his black slave? The engraving fully succeeds at neither, thus forcing the reader to ponder the reason for the apparent deviation.

As a way of obliquely answering this question, William interjects an important assertion on behalf of his wife: "My wife had no ambition whatever to assume this disguise, and would not have done so had it been possible to have obtained our liberty by more simple means; but we knew it was not customary in the South for ladies to travel with male servants; and therefore, notwithstanding my wife's fair complexion, it would have been a very difficult task for her to come off as a free white lady, with me as her slave" (*RTMF* 35). In many ways, this is reflective of the anxiety accompanying the other kinds of border crossings in the text, though in this case the anxiety is William's in relation to his wife's gender transgression. This becomes a reflection of a kind of desire on William's part to exert some type of narrative control and insert some way for the reader to distinguish between choice and necessity. William's wife, otherwise an embodiment of true womanhood, actively chooses to mask that womanhood in favor of a momentary necessity to step beyond the boundaries of her "true" role in favor of a white masculine forgery.[14]

Ellen is for William ultimately a wife who creates anxiety for her husband when she situationally crosses the boundaries of race, class, and gender and seemingly dominates the rhetorical control William has textually established for himself. But the rhetorical mastery that William creates for himself is not reflected in his actual life. In reality, William continues (at that moment, at least) to be the "property" of the slaveowner from whom he is escaping. During their escape, William becomes the "property" of a master who is also his wife. While it is not clear whether William sees this reversal as a kind of emasculation, it is clear that these role inversions speak toward the jeopardized order requiring the clearly defined social positions the narrative assaults. The apparent discomfort that surfaces may, however, have less to do with William's insecurity concerning his wife or the roles she plays. It potentially has much more to do with a discomfort William feels in his relationship with his reader and the kinds of circumstances the reader has anticipated before reading the narrative.

Illustration 5.1. Ellen Craft in her disguise. Frontispiece of
Running a Thousand Miles for Freedom.

The narrative tension inscribed in their escape attempt is based on Ellen's "readers" (those whom she encounters during her journey) accepting her ruse. Similarly, the unsettled (and unsettling) portion of the narrative in which William refers to his wife as "master" and her gender as "he" requires the reader of the narrative similarly to accept the rhetorical ruse the narrative performs. Thus, the mastery described in the relationship of a master and a slave is not as fully reflected in the illusory relationship between Ellen and her "slave" William as it is in the rhetorical mastery William achieves over his reader. William notes, for example, that immediately upon arriving in Philadelphia and satisfying themselves that they had achieved their freedom, Ellen "threw off the disguise and assumed her own apparel" (*RTMF* 81). William will have the reader believe that Ellen has no desire to continue to maintain the control she has temporarily gained over her husband.

During the escape, Ellen serves as William's "protection," thus bringing to mind the "protections" Frederick Douglass wrote to help the members of his group pass from slavery into freedom. Ellen's role is similarly textual inasmuch as she serves as the focal and thematic center of the narrative's extended escape episode. The ability of the narrative to move and persuade a potentially skeptical reader is at the heart of William's discomfort. William's desire to manipulate how slavery is understood through his mediation of how the reader is allowed to access Ellen is at the heart of his anxiety. The kind of tension that is maintained between William (the slave) and Ellen (the master) during the escape portion of the narrative suggests a doubleness between William, who maintains his "voice," and Ellen, whose "voice" is largely taken from her as a precaution against giving away her gender. Yet Ellen, as the transgressive figure, is the one who becomes the subject of William's gaze and William's "voice." William's difficulty is in simultaneously maintaining his position as a participant in the scheme and as an active observer.

William's function almost becomes anthropological in the sense that his involvement and emotional identification are integral to the process of describing experience and meaning. At the same time, he is restricted by the literal distance he is required to keep from his "master" and the figurative distance he must maintain in order adequately to record and evaluate the process. William and Ellen become representatives of a kind of exterior self-division in which they become superimposed, complementary examples of subject and object, slave and master, black and white. As Ellen passes across a number of geographic, racial, and gendered borders, the narrative becomes representative of the difficulty in adequately maintaining equilibrium in the matrix of hybrid insubstantiality of William's position of author-observer and, momentarily at least, his redefined position in relation to his "master" Ellen, who becomes the focal point of his inquiring gaze.

In my discussion of Frederick Douglass's *Narrative*, I noted that Douglass himself creates a voyeuristic environment containing the description of an overseer named Mr. Plummer, who cruelly whips his Aunt Hester. Douglass writes that "I remember the first time I ever witnessed this horrible exhibition. I was quite a child, but I well remember it. I never shall forget it whilst I remember any thing. It was the first of a long series of such outrages, of which I was doomed to be a witness and a participant. It struck me with awful force. It was the blood-stained gate, the entrance to the hell of slavery, through which I was about to pass. It was a most terrible spectacle. I wish I could commit to paper the feelings with which I beheld it" (*N* 18). Douglass, and by extension, his reader, is forced voyeuristically to gaze at a spectacle that cannot adequately be conquered even through the act of writing. Douglass is ultimately unable to completely serve the role of bystander or detached participant who serves a writerly function. For Douglass, there is no either/or construction: He cannot be either the witness or the participant, the writer or the subject of the writer's gaze because fate has consigned him to the role of being both "a witness and a participant." The act of splitting these two roles is not an advantage available to him.

In constructing his story, William does have the option of simultaneously giving words to the experience. He does this even as he becomes a kind of indifferent, detached spectator, much like the other disinterested observers who are duped by Ellen's disguise. The ability to give words to the experience allows William to assume a certain level of mastery and authority. Hence, at the outset of their escape, when he begins to refer to Ellen as his "master," William is transformed into an observer gazing at his "master" from the confines of the "negro car." The split between the two roles William and Ellen occupy creates an opportunity to explore the systems of slavery, dominance, and racial identity that the text seeks to examine. As he has sought to do in the section of the narrative preceding their escape attempt, William's focus, now worked through the split consciousness he and Ellen assume, engages the concept of white identity and self-examination in direct relation to culturally inscribed beliefs about blackness.

In *Playing the Dark* (1992), her Du Boisian meditation on the constructions of "literary whiteness" and "literary blackness," Toni Morrison examines the ways in which literary representations of "individualism, masculinity, social engagement versus historical isolation; acute and ambiguous moral problematics; the thematics of innocence coupled with an obsession with figurations of death and hell—are not in fact responses to a dark, abiding, signing Africanist presence."[15] For Morrison, the Africanist presence was crucial to the sense of Americanness white Americans had of themselves. In the case of the narrative created by William and Ellen Craft in *Running a Thousand Miles for Freedom*, an act of collective, racial self-authentication (as opposed to the kinds of individualized authorizing strategies at work in the other fugitive slave stories discussed here) takes place when Ellen assumes her disguise. Ellen becomes a white man who is a member of the slaveholding class who is accompanied by her "slave" William (who also serves as the author-observer of Ellen's activities). She offers her reader an occasion to see the ways in which white maleness is indebted (in terms of William's function as the one who constructs and mediates the text) to the visual presence and conception of black masculinity. Taken as a unit, the escape of William and Ellen Craft requires them simultaneously to see, in the case of William, and be seen, in the case of Ellen.

During a tenuous moment in their escape, Ellen, who is unable to write, is asked to sign her name in the registry of a steamer bound from Charleston, South Carolina, to Wilmington, North Carolina. William writes, "My master paid the dollar, and pointing to the hand that was in the poultice, requested the officer to register his name for him. This seemed to offend the 'high-bred' South Carolinian" (*RTMF* 56), who refused. In this instance, Ellen and William have momentarily misread the codes of conduct attached to class rather than race. Their plan is saved by the fortuitous arrival of a drunk young military officer with whom Ellen had traveled. William notes that "he shook hands with my master, and pretended to know all about him. He said, 'I know his kin (friends) like a book;' and as the officer was known in Charleston, and was going to stop there with friends, the recognition was very much in my master's favour" (*RTMF* 56–57). The ironic humor William uses in describing the moment is undeniable: "When the gentleman finds out his mistake, he will, I have no doubt, be careful in future not to pretend to have an intimate acquaintance with an entire stranger" (*RTMF* 57). Here, Ellen is not merely consigned to the stock role of "Aunt" or "Uncle" that was so much a part of plantation culture. (In a footnote later in the text, William notes that "I may state here that every man is called boy till he is very old, then the more respectable slaveholders call him uncle. The women are all girls till they are aged, then they are called aunts" [*RTMF* 77].) By accepting Ellen as a white man, the young military officer mistakenly offers Ellen-as-Mr. Johnson entry into the extended familial social relationship that characterized pre-Civil War southern society. William's decision to include this story suggests his desire to rewrite the text of the southern family that includes black aunts and uncles in favor of a revised way of seeing and understanding black experience.

It is the presence of a new understanding of blackness (embodied in the existence of Ellen-as-Mr. Johnson) that foreshadows the arrival of the post-Reconstruction New Negro and, more emphatically, the tensions created by the rise of a New Negro in the 1890s. What the narrative consistently shows (here and in other passages when white travelers warn Mr. Johnson of the danger of treating his slave humanely and of taking him into northern territory) is that the white race fuses itself into a homogeneous mass of connection and shared self-interest based entirely upon whiteness. If the lines between black and white or male and female are effectively obscured in the context of William and Ellen's ruse, so too are the lines of national ancestry, class distinction, and even social connection. William creates an essentialist view of whiteness that is bound as much by Ellen's skin color as by the social and political concerns that connect Ellen-as-Mr. Johnson to other whites. White readers of *Running a Thousand Miles for Freedom* would be forced into a new awareness of their racial identity because Ellen's experiences chronicle an overturning of racial identity structured on the foundation of some kind of inherent racial superiority. On both sides of the equation, white and black, the narrative invokes essentialist views of race and gender as a way of making an easy view of binary, essentialist, hierarchical definitions ultimately unworkable. The borders of definition *between* the areas of definition are virtually as impossible to police as the areas *within* those definitions that are so murky and undefined. What morally undermines the South (and, in the years following the Civil War, will undermine the ability of the South adequately to address social and cultural developments in the nation as a whole) is a strict adherence to racial determinism.

William similarly directs an ironic humor toward others who mis-read Ellen-as-Mr. Johnson. While traveling on a train, a gentleman questions Ellen-as-Mr. Johnson about his affliction. After being told that inflammatory rheumatism is the cause of Ellen-as-Mr. Johnson's discomfort, he remarks that "I can sympathise with you; for I know from bitter experience what rheumatism is," to which William notes "If he did, he knew a good deal more than Mr. Johnson" (*RTMF* 59). The daughters of the gentleman are similarly duped by Ellen-as-Mr. Johnson and are also the recipients of William's ironic commentary. When one of the gentleman's daughters remarks that "I never felt so much for a gentleman in my life!," William notes that "To use an American expression, 'they fell in love with the wrong chap' " (*RTMF* 60). In this instance, the comment obviously plays upon a concern about trans-gender identification. But in the larger context of the nar-rative, the comments (in conjunction with William's ironic commen-tary) also speaks toward a hybridization of circumstances that can se-lectively include various aspects of race, class, and gender.

Ellen is circumstantially required by the design of the masquerade to become, at a number of levels, the Other. Yet she never entirely surrenders her sense of herself in the charade. As a matter of fact, as soon as William and Ellen safely arrive in the North, William notes that "After my wife had a little recovered herself, she threw off the disguise and assumed her own apparel" (*RTMF* 81). There is no sense of idealized conclusion after the escape or at the close of the narrative. Ellen seems to have no desire to live on the borders of the color line. She uses her miscegenated status to offer a fundamental reinterpreta-tion of America's cultural assumptions. The narrative asks its readers to examine the perception of essentialized white racial pureness and superiority (and the corresponding belief in black inferiority) in terms of the historical and legal lies upon which these beliefs are based.

The central question directing this book has to do with how slave narrators authorize themselves within the context of the narrow space in which their story is culturally confined. In terms of *Running a Thousand Miles for Freedom*, this returns the reader to the unresolved issue of exactly who it is who is being represented and authorized in the text. Part I of the narrative, which details the background, formu-lation, and execution of their plan, naturally focuses fairly directly on Ellen. Yet, as I have noted, Ellen's "voice" is mediated by William's narrative control and presentation. Similarly, William's presence in the first part of the narrative is primarily confined to offering narrative context for their actions and recording Ellen's experiences as she passes for his master.

Ultimately, the narrative does not attempt to resolve the tensions it addresses. The narrative becomes a kind of bellwether for the many ambiguous models of race, gender, and class the Crafts' experiences invoke. As the narrator of his and his wife's shared experience, one of William's options in constructing their story is to become the kind of former slave Frederick Douglass becomes when he equates "voice" with self-presentation. Given the obviously subversive context of their story, William also has the opportunity to authorize himself and Ellen as the engineers of a new role that will force them both to accept the results of their radical self-re-invention. But William ignores both of these options of closure in favor of the standard fugitive slave story resolution, which denies that he has narrated the most horrible of slave experiences: "In the preceding pages I have not dwelt upon the great barbarities which are practised upon the slaves; because I wish to present the system in its mildest form, and to show that the 'tender mercies of the wicked are cruel' " (*RTMF* 110–11). This closing sounds remarkably unresolved and ambiguous in relation to the intensely transgressive, focused quality of the escape itself.

William offers a standard resolution to the narrative, but the resolution of the issues he has raised are firmly returned to the hands of his readers. Almost deceptively, William uses a traditional rhetorical device for ending the narrative and relies on traditional paradigms of black victimhood and white responsibility. But the ostensibly obvious distinctions the narrative makes at its conclusion regarding the apparent moral culpability of the reader subverts the ways in which the narrative itself, especially the escape episode, undermines any attempts essentially to define race, class, or gender. The unambiguously binary conclusion of the text stands in stark contrast to the ambiguous relations and definitions the first part of the text calls into question. Thus, while the conclusion of the narrative employs the form, language, and imagery of the antislavery agenda, the narrative itself suggests that Ellen (in terms of physical representation) and William (in terms of literary representation) each has the capacity to capture the rhetorical control and authority that allows them momentarily to become that which they are not.

Of Being and Nothingness:
Caliban's Reprise

Memory believes before knowing remembers. Believes longer
than recollects, longer than knowing even wonders.
—William Faulkner, *Light in August*

If you want Negro history you will have to get it from
somebody who wore the shoe, and by and by from one
to the other you will get a book.
—former slave, Fisk Collection,
Unwritten History of Slavery

I BEGAN this book by invoking images contained in the distance
between memory and knowing, expectation and actuality. As I
have suggested, the success of the fugitive slave story as a genre
is ostensibly a function of how well narrators manipulated the cultural
hierarchy of forms and images made available to them. But contemporary critical models that depend on engaging the narratives in terms
of the obvious areas of oppositional forms (like black and white or
slave and free) that the narratives employ will continue to interpret
the narratives in ways that are ultimately limiting. The narratives
themselves will continue to refute attempts at seeing them in ways
that require them to be readily viewed as autobiography, history,
truth, or fiction. At the very least, the narratives require a style of
reading that acknowledges that they are the product of a series of
oppositional forces that, even for the narrators themselves, are elastic
in their influence and meaning.

For the narrators represented here, the authorial consciousness and
awareness they bring to the creation of their stories suggests the ways
racial politics simultaneously intrude upon and structure, endanger,
and nourish their understanding and presentation of their individual
consciousness. The very focus of the stories of fugitive slaves suggests
that there is an inherent estrangement between the impulse to tell the

story of a life and the reality that the interest of the story for the reader is in the partial (that is, the events precipitating the escape and the escape itself). Thus, to say that the fugitive slave story is a strongly mediated form is a truism. What is considerably less obvious is that the intense mediation of the form brings with it a great deal of displacement. In seeking to authorize a place for themselves, fugitive slave narrators end up telling their own stories (and creating meaning) by essentially telling the stories of others; the individual life presented within the story is very much a function of the collective stories of all who contribute to the black experience.

The notion of "voice" has been central to my approach, as have discussions of the gaze and mirroring. There is, however, no easy correspondence when issues of identity, especially racial identity, are involved. As a consequence of this, the reflections are often skewed and distorted.[1] These comments speak most directly toward the idea of the gaze and the anxiety attached to the act of correctly reading the reality of the identity behind the mask. These thoughts also have an application to the fact that for African Americans, both discovering and creating a "voice" becomes the function of a performative requirement focusing on mediation and misdirection. There is neither an objective authority nor an essential identity. Neither is there a realistic possibility of simply replacing one aspect of identity with another. Hence the inherent complications of "voice" and disguise. In this context, the rhetorical act of telling one's story is much more a reflection of the writer's desire to compose and authorize an experience and much less a linear act of recalling and ordering experience.

The act of establishing a "voice" requires that the former slave storyteller negotiate the sometimes overlapping need for personal as well as literary survival. The commonly accepted belief that literacy alone is sufficient for attaining freedom is consistently shown to be incorrect by the submerged meaning contained in many of the stories themselves. Frederick Douglass, for example, is perhaps most emphatic in articulating his growing awareness of the connection between literacy and freedom. In opposition to his master, Mr. Auld, Douglass makes the famous remark that "That which to him was a great evil to be carefully shunned, was to me a great good, to be diligently sought; and the argument which he so warmly urged, against my learning to read, only served to inspire me with a desire and determination to learn" (*N* 38). But the *Narrative* indicates that reading and writing were not necessarily the keys to freedom and the tools that would provide Douglass the opportunity to redefine his links to the authority that he had envisioned. They were, conversely, the keys to a deeper enslavement. His ability to read eventually became for him a "curse" and the ability to write (indicated by the "protections" Douglass forges for the group's failed escape attempt, whose words they must eat in order to keep their escape plans from being discovered) ends up getting him imprisoned. Similarly, the letters Linda Brent writes from her hiding place in the crawlspace of her grandmother's house and arranges to have sent to her master, Dr. Flint, from the North indicates a similar play on the apparent disparity between literacy and either rhetorical or physical freedom.

Each of these attempts, and the very existence of the stories themselves, suggests an awareness on the part of the former-slave narrator of the subtle ways in which language is itself the essence of institutional and cultural power and authority. These narrators create their stories from a point of origin where they have been effectively obscured. They are required first to succeed in finding and establishing a "voice" before proceeding to the business of establishing an interpretive stance. Their human circumstance therefore becomes synonymous with their literary circumstance. Former-slave narrators see their lives as an unreconciled fusion of presence and nonexistence simultaneously shaped and negated by cultural attitudes deeply seated in racial image.[2]

In addressing the ways in which fugitive slave narrative writers sought to authorize themselves, I have indirectly invoked the dual issues of commodity and consumption.[3] For fugitive slave narrators, the actions of a social agenda that consumed their experiences essentially did so by offering a possibility of success contingent upon their ability to convince their readership to consume and assimilate slave experience altered in relation to that audience's own sense of themselves. What is especially astonishing about the popularity of narratives by former slaves is that they were commodified and consumed almost as completely in a literary context as the narrators were physically consumed as slaves.[4]

As I have noted elsewhere, the visual element is integral to my reading of the narratives. The implication of this reading is necessarily reliant upon a framework informed by rhetorical figurations of "race" and experience instead of individual, racially defined experience. By seeing the narratives as being generically concerned with showing the ways black identity was a cultural fabrication, narratives ostensibly concerned with personal experience become, when seen in a generic context that is strongly informed by racial stereotype and cultural assumptions about blackness, transformed into illustrations of self-authorized character. My intention has been to argue for a means of addressing the narratives that acknowledges the ways former-slave narrators sought to authorize and create themselves in the literary recitation of their stories.

More than anything, my reading of fugitive slave stories argues that those stories offer testimony in all of the many and varied meanings of that word. Fugitive slave narrators testified to their experiences of slavery and their efforts to escape. The stories themselves testify to the literary efforts of the writers to reorient themselves as not only the social focus of southern oppression and the literary center of adventurous stories of escape but also to take for themselves a subjective, authorial role that allows them to interpret their experiences and rhetorically situate those experiences within a larger context of culture and meaning. In offering testimony, fugitive slave narrators also implicate their reader. The reader does not offer testimony, yet it is the reader to whom the narrator testifies. Positioned as a kind of jury, the reader offers judgment. Lastly, fugitive slave narrators testify in a way that is reflected in the context of African-American religious experience. In this meaning of the word, the person offering testimony addresses a gathering and gives a chronicle of experience, faith, and hope. The experiences described are necessarily personal, individual experiences. The story is offered in the spirit of faith and self-revelation such that individual experience finds resonance with the audience to whom it is conveyed. The revelation of experience, seen from one perspective as personal and individual, serves as a bridge between the individual and the communal. Experience transcends individuality and addresses the commonality of identity, and especially black identity, as a cultural fabrication.

At a time when American writers like James Fenimore Cooper, William Gilmore Simms, Ralph Waldo Emerson, Nathaniel Hawthorne, Herman Melville, and Walt Whitman were struggling to find a form of literary expression that could be seen as being distinctly "American," fugitive slave narrators, in writing their stories—speaking for themselves—created literature that was itself uniquely "American." It attempted to utilize a form that was adaptable enough simultaneously to discuss the American issues of freedom and identity upon which the republic had built its liberal democratic ideals. From its very origins, the New World sought to define itself as a place where the individual—the American Adam—could create a self capable of defining and reconciling the variousness of his or her origins and create for that persona a unique place in the world. But African Americans—the American Jeremiahs—were rarely, even in the case of free blacks, given access to similar resources and assumptions. Yet they were able somehow to merge collective experience with individual hopes and ambitions and in the process create writing as thoroughly "American" as the work of any of those writers usually associated with that phenomenon.

Africans and the American descendants of those Africans are buried there. In their stories. In their words.

NOTES

INTRODUCTION
THE LITERARY MASKS OF FUGITIVE SLAVE STORIES

1. Robbins, "Gendering the History of the Antislavery Narrative," 531–33; Davidson, *Revolution and the Word*, 3–14, 15–37.

2. Sundquist, *To Wake the Nations*, 38–40.

3. Stepto, *From Behind the Veil*, 4–31, esp. 6.

4. Roper, *A Narrative of the Adventures and Escape of Moses Roper*, vi.

5. Roper, *A Narrative of the Adventures and Escape of Moses Roper*, iv.

6. Gates, Jr., "Binary Oppositions in Chapter One of *Narrative of the Life of Frederick Douglass an American Slave Written by Himself*," 85–86; Levi-Strauss, *Totemism*, 130; Jameson, *The Prison-House of Language*, 113; Jakobson and Halle, *Fundamentals of Language*, 4, 47–49; Du Bois, *The Souls of Black Folk*, 37–44.

7. Du Bois, *The Souls of Black Folk*, 37.

8. Du Bois, *The Souls of Black Folk*, 38.

9. Du Bois, *The Souls of Black Folk*, 38.

10. Du Bois, *The Souls of Black Folk*, 38.

11. Williams, *The Alchemy of Race and Rights*, 44–46. See also Marcus, "Theories of Autobiography," 21–22.

12. Du Bois, *The Souls of Black Folk*, 38.

13. Du Bois, *The Souls of Black Folk*, 39.

14. Du Bois, *The Souls of Black Folk*, 38.

15. In *Harlem Renaissance*, Nathan Irvin Huggins writes, in direct response to Du Bois's thoughts on "double-consciousness," that "This remarkable and profound statement fails only to make explicit an important corollary: this 'double-consciousness' open to the Negro—through his own quest and passion—a unique insight into the vulnerable and unfulfilled soul of that other world; a possibility which, once grasped, liberates one forever from the snarls of that other world's measuring tape" (244–45). See also Gates, Jr., *The Signifying Monkey*, Awkward, *Inspiriting Influences*, Baker, Jr., *Long Black Song* and *Modernism and the Harlem Renaissance*; and Hale, "Bakhtin in African American Theory," esp. 448–61, who very effectively reads Du Bois's thoughts on "double-consciousness" in relation to Bakhtin's theory of "double-voiced discourse" and argues that "Bakhtin's description of language as a container for multiple social identities means that the invasion of the African American's physical body can be countered by the African American's own invasion of the hegemonic linguistic body" (460).

16. Carby, *Reconstructing Womanhood*, 151.

17. Huggins, *Harlem Renaissance*, 261.

18. A number of recent studies have approached the subject of African-American narrative writing in general and of slave narrative writing in particular. To varying degrees, these studies have each accepted the metaphor of doubleness and have sought to reconcile that metaphor as a useful tool for examining the African-American experience. These investigations include Stepto, *From Behind the Veil*; Smith, *Self-Discovery and Authority in Afro-American Narrative*; Braxton, *Black Women Writing Autobiography*; Gates, Jr., *Figures in Black* and *The Signifying Monkey*; Andrews, *To Tell a Free Story*; Awkward, *Inspiriting Influences*; Baker, Jr., *Long Black Song* and *Modernism and the Harlem Renaissance*; Callahan, *In the African-American Grain*; Jones, *Liberating Voices*; Butler-Evans, *Race, Gender, and Desire*.

19. Gates, Jr., ed., *Six Women's Slave Narratives*, xxxii.

20. Baker, Jr., *Singers of Daybreak*, 9; Foster, "Neither Auction Block nor Pedestal," 144–45.

21. Yee, *Black Women Abolitionists*, 112–35, esp. 112–15.

22. Stephen Greenblatt notes that "A literary criticism that has affinities to this practice [cultural criticism] must be conscious of its own status as interpretation and intent upon understanding literature as a part of the system of signs that constitutes a given culture; its proper goal, however difficult to realize, is a *poetics of culture* [italics in original]" (*Renaissance Self-Fashioning*, 4).

23. Ellison, "Blues People," 278–87; Morrison, "Unspeakable Things Unspoken," 18.

CHAPTER 1
THE CULTURAL CONTEXT

1. Bakhtin, "Discourse in the Novel," 293.

2. Wright, *12 Million Black Voices*, 40.

3. Wright, *12 Million Black Voices*, 1–5.

4. Ring, "Painting by Numbers," 134–35.

5. hooks, *Black Looks*, 2–7, 165–78; Hall, "Cultural Identity and Diaspora," 225–26.

6. Morrison, ed., *Race-ing Justice, En-gendering Power*, xxviii–xxix.

7. Cheyfitz notes that "When Caliban responds to Miranda in what are by now quite famous lines: 'You taught me language; and my profit on't / Is, I know how to curse' (I. ii. 365–66), we might well notice a certain irony in the lines. For there is no profit for Caliban in learning the Europeans' language; though he knows how to curse, he does not know how to curse in the eloquent, or lethal, manner of his master" (Cheyfitz, *The Poetics of Imperialism*, 34).

8. Hedin, "The American Slave Narrative," 631, 645.

9. Kibbey, "Language in Slavery," 143–45. See also Rawick, *From Sundown to Sunup*, 6–10, who correctly notes that "Human society is a cumulate process in which the past is never totally obliterated. Even revolutions do not destroy the past. Indeed, at their best, they liberate that which is alive from that which stifles human progress,

growth, and development. Culture is a historical reality, not an ahistorical, static abstraction. Thus, the process whereby the African in the New World changed in order to meet his new environment was dependent upon his African culture. While it is certainly true that the African under American slavery changed, he did so in ways that were recognizably African" (Rawick, *From Sundown to Sunup*, 6).

10. Graham, "Black Letters; or Uncle Tom-Foolery in Literature," 209.

11. Including, for example, *A Narrative of the Uncommon Sufferings, and Surprizing Deliverance of Briton Hammon, a Negro Man* (1760); *A Narrative of the Most Remarkable Particulars in the Life of James Albert Ukawsaw Gronniosaw* (1770); *The Narrative of the Lord's Wonderful Dealings with John Marrant* (1785); *The Interesting Narrative of the Life of Olaudah Equiano, or Gustavus Vassa, the African. Written by Himself* (1789).

12. Gibson, *The Politics of Literary Expression*, 3–13. He notes, for example, that "Most black writers of the past and of the present write with an eye to the social situation of the time in which they are writing. With few exceptions, black writers have produced literature that reflects their situations as social beings existing within a particular historical framework and subject to the pressures of a special nature resulting therefrom" (Gibson, *The Politics of Literary Expression*, 4).

13. Gayle, Jr., *The Way of the New World*, xii.

14. Pascal, *Design and Truth in Autobiography*, 1–3; Olney, " 'I Was Born,' " 149.

15. Blassingame, "Using the Testimony of Ex-Slaves," 78–98.

16. Marcus, "Theories of Autobiography," 20–22; Felman, *What Does a Woman Want?*," 14–19, 148–51, 155–56n. 16; Felman and Laub, *Testimony*, 5.

17. Pascal, *Design and Truth in Autobiography*, 15–16.

18. Olney, " 'I Was Born,' " 154; Smith, *Self-Discovery and Authority in Afro-American Narrative*, 9–12.

19. Costanzo, *Surprizing Narrative*, 17.

20. Olney, " 'I Was Born,' " 154; Costanzo, *Surprizing Narrative*, 15–17.

21. Niemtzow, "The Problematic Self in Autobiography," 107–8.

22. Cox, "Autobiography and America," 254.

23. Andrews, *To Tell a Free Story*, 19 and 296n. 37.

24. Pascal, *Design and Truth in Autobiography*, especially 83, 188; Renza, "The Veto of the Imagination," 268–70.

25. Stepto, in *From Behind the Veil*, 3, argues that the term "slave narrative" is an umbrella term encompassing many different kinds of narratives, a point with which I largely agree. But while my view of the slave narrative focuses on what I see as the fluid continuum of cultural contexts that shaped the genre, Stepto confines his focus to the various authenticating documents surrounding individual narratives and argues for a rubric that divides the narrative tradition into three artificially rigid, distinct phases: the "Eclectic Narrative," with authenticating documents appended to the tale; the "Integrated Narrative," with authenticating credentials incorporated into the tale; and the third phase, which he splits into the "Generic Narrative," where

the narrative becomes identifiably autobiographical, and the "Authenticating Narrative," where the narrative authenticates another text, like a novel.

26. Cox, "Autobiography and America," 252–55.

27. Kazin, "Autobiography as Narrative," 210–13.

28. Cox, "Autobiography and America," 255–58.

29. Olney, " 'I Was Born,' " 152–56.

<h2 style="text-align:center">CHAPTER 2</h2>

THE LIMITATIONS OF "VOICE" IN *THE CONFESSIONS* OF *NAT TURNER*

1. Turner, *The Confessions of Nat Turner and Related Documents*, 40. All subsequent references to the text appear parenthetically as *CNT*.

2. For a fuller understanding of Turner himself, see Tragle, *The Southampton Slave Revolt of 1831*; Aptheker, *Nat Turner's Slave Rebellion*.

3. Sundquist, *To Wake the Nations*, 46–47.

4. Garrison, *William Lloyd Garrison*, I, 134–35; quoted in Abzug, "The Influence of Garrisonian Abolitionists' Fears of Slave Violence on the Antislavery Argument," 15.

5. Letter of Mrs. James Boyle, printed in *The Liberator*, April 5, 1839, 56. See also Demos, "The Antislavery Movement and the Problem of Violent 'Means'," 514.

6. *The Liberator*, January 8, 1831.

7. *The Liberator*, May 14, 1839; quoted in Abzug, "The Influence of Garrison Abolitionists' Fears," 20 (emphasis added).

8. My description of Samuel Turner and his attitudes toward his slaves is largely drawn from Oates, *The Fires of Jubilee*, 8–13.

9. Tragle, *The Southampton Slave Revolt of 1831*, 221–23; Fabricant, "Thomas R. Gray and William Styron," 343–44.

10. Tragle, *The Southampton Slave Revolt of 1831*, 402.

11. Fabricant, "Thomas R. Gray and William Styron," 342–43.

12. Andrews, *To Tell a Free Story*, 72.

13. Andrews argues that "Gray knew that in Turner's own deposition he would explain and justify his actions on the basis of scriptural precedent, divine revelation, and conscientious adherence to his perception of the will of God. Before Turner could occupy that sacred ground rhetorically, Gray tried to deny him a tropological avenue by introducing a countertrope that would turn the reader's thinking significance in a direction opposite from that in which Turner would try to take it" (*To Tell a Free Story*, 74).

14. Fabricant, "Thomas R. Gray and William Styron," 339–40; Sundquist, *To Wake the Nations*, 46–47; Tragle, *The Southampton Slave Revolt of 1831*, 402–9.

15. Luke 12: 31, "But rather seek ye the kingdom of God; and all these things shall be added unto you."

16. Matthew 19: 30, "But many that are first shall be last; and the last shall be first"; Matthew 20: 16, "So the last shall be first, and the first last: for many be called, but few chosen"; Mark 10: 31, "But many that are first shall be last; and the last first"; Luke 13: 30, "And behold, there are last which shall be first, and there are first which shall be last."

17. Andrews, *To Tell a Free Story*, 74–75.

18. Andrews, "Inter(racial)textuality in Nineteenth-Century Southern Litera-ture," 304.

19. Sundquist argues that "With no doubt some isolated exceptions of complete subservience to the rule of slavery, Nat Turner *was* in every family, whether he acted out his violent impulses or not" (*To Wake the Nations*, 54); see also Elkins, *Slavery*, 89–103; Rawick, *From Sundown to Sunup*, 95–96.

20. Sundquist, *To Wake the Nations*, 52–54.

21. Sundquist, *To Wake the Nations*, 83.

22. Andrews, "Inter(racial)textuality in Nineteenth-Century Southern Narrative," 303–5.

23. Turner, *The Confessions of Nat Turner*, 27.

24. Stepto, *From Behind the Veil*, 3.

CHAPTER 3
SACRED LANGUAGE AND THE SECULAR SELF IN FREDERICK DOUGLASS'S *NARRATIVE*

1. O'Meally, "The Text Was Meant to Be Preached," 77–94. See also Ann Kibbey and Michele Stepto, "The Antilanguage of Slavery"; Donald B. Gibson, "Faith, Doubt, and Apostasy"; and Thad Ziolkowski, "Antithesis."

2. Quoted in Starling, *The Slave Narrative*, 19.

3. In her groundbreaking examination of slave narrative writing, Marion Wilson Starling even goes so far as to assert that along with increasing secular debate regarding slavery and escalating southern entrenchment in the slave system, the abolition of slavery in the West Indies in 1834 brought an influx of overseers from what is generally considered one of the more brutal slave systems. Though it seems difficult to substantiate, she argues that the influx in the South of this kind of thinking about slavery created the kind of harsher American system that is reflected in scenes of vio-lence that appear as standard episodes in subsequent fugitive slave narratives. See Starling, *The Slave Narrative*, 29.

4. Douglass, *Narrative*, 119. All subsequent references to the text appear paren-thetically as *N*.

5. Kibbey and Stepto, "The Antilanguage of Slavery," 167–68.

6. Kibbey and Stepto, "The Antilanguage of Slavery," 167.

7. O'Meally, "The Text Was Meant to Be Preached," 82.

8. Goddu and Smith, "Scenes of Writing in Frederick Douglass's *Narrative*," 822–23.

9. Ngũgĩ, *Moving the Centre*, 32.

10. Hawley, "We Wretched of the Earth," 135; During, "Postmodernism or post-colonialism today," 43; Ngũgĩ, *Moving the Centre*, 32.

11. Callahan, *In the African American Grain*, 25–30.

12. Foster, *Witnessing Slavery*, 56–57.

13. Quoted in Aptheker, *Abolitionism*, 65.

14. Aptheker, *Abolitionism*, 65–66.

15. Quoted in *ibid.*, 66.

16. Du Bois, *The Souls of Black Folk*, 38.

17. Martin, *The Mind of Frederick Douglass*, 196–202.

18. Gates, Jr., "Binary Oppositions," 89–91; Rowe, "Between Politics and Poetics," 203–6.

19. Rowe, "Between Politics and Poetics," 204–6.

20. Gates, Jr., "Binary Oppositions," 89–90; Rowe, "Between Politics and Poetics," 203–6.

21. Martin, *The Mind of Frederick Douglass*, 200–202; Brotz, ed., *Negro Social and Political Thought*, 290; Fredrickson, *The Black Image in the White Mind*, 97–129.

22. Fredrickson, *The Black Image in the White Mind*, 97–107.

23. Stowe, *Uncle Tom's Cabin*, xiii.

24. Carson, "Shaking the Foundation," 20–21; Van Leer, "Reading Slavery," 118–19.

25. Though Douglass did not escape by way of the Chesapeake, he did disguise himself as a sailor, pretend to be free, and travel north by train.

26. Carson, "Shaking the Foundation," 26–27.

27. Warhol, " 'Reader, Can You Imagine? No, You Cannot,' " 66–67.

28. Baker, Jr., *Blues, Ideology and Afro-American Literature*, 46–47; Carson, "Shaking the Foundation," 28.

29. Van Leer, "Reading Slavery," 118–19.

30. Carson, "Shaking the Foundation," 28–29.

31. Van Leer, "Reading Slavery," 125–26.

32. Van Leer, "Reading Slavery," 120–23.

33. Douglass, in *My Bondage and My Freedom*, is considerably less cryptic about whom he and his co-conspirators suspect of revealing their plan to escape: "Master Thomas would not tell us *who* his informant was; but we suspected, and suspected *one* person *only*. Several circumstances seemed to point Sandy out, as our betrayer. His entire knowledge of our plans—his participation in them—his withdrawal from us—his dream, and his simultaneous presentiment that we were betrayed—the taking us, and the leaving him—were calculated to turn suspicion toward him; and yet, we could not suspect him. We all loved him too well to think it *possible* that he could have betrayed us. So we rolled the guilt on other shoulders" (*MBMF* 321). These sentiments are consistent with Douglass's apparent objective in *My Bondage and My Freedom* to deepen the sense of relationship and human connection that in the *Narrative* is often minimized in favor of his pursuit of freedom and his desire to individualize himself.

CHAPTER 4
THE DILEMMA OF RHETORICAL OWNERSHIP IN FREDERICK DOUGLASS'S
MY BONDAGE AND MY FREEDOM AND HARRIET JACOBS'S *INCIDENTS
IN THE LIFE OF A SLAVE GIRL*

1. Gates, Jr., "Binary Oppositions in Chapter One of *Narrative of the Life of Frederick Douglass an American Slave Written by Himself*," 85–87.

2. Sundquist sees Douglass's revision of his life as "the sign of his embrace of the principles of autonomy, property, and equal rights" (*To Wake the Nations*, 89).

3. Andrews, *To Tell a Free Story*, 218–19.

4. Douglass, *My Bondage and My Freedom*, 125. All subsequent references to the text appear parenthetically as *MBMF*.

5. Andrews, *To Tell a Free Story*, 233.

6. Dorsey, "Becoming the Other," 439–40.

7. Sekora, " 'Mr. Editor, If You Please,' " 622–23.

8. Martin, *The Mind of Frederick Douglass*, 56–58.

9. Sekora, " 'Mr. Editor, If You Please,' " 624–25.

10. Sundquist sees this shift as indicating Douglass's desire that his reader see this moment as the initiation of his public self rather than as the culmination of his experiences as a slave (*To Wake the Nations*, 87–88).

11. Bakhtin, "Discourse in the Novel," 277.

12. Sundquist, *To Wake the Nations*, 90.

13. Sundquist, *To Wake the Nations*, 90.

14. Clarke, *Narratives of the Sufferings of Lewis and Milton Clarke*, 102–24.

15. Andrews, *To Tell a Free Story*, 236.

16. Wilson J. Moses, "Writing Freely?," 80, notes that the successive versions of Douglass's narratives, beginning with the *Narrative* (1845) and including *My Bondage and My Freedom* (1855), *The Life and Times of Frederick Douglass* (1882), and the revised version of *The Life and Times of Frederick Douglass* (1892), indicate his increasing desire to move beyond the boundaries of race, which he had already overstepped because of his biracial parentage, and toward the nonracialized world suggested by the title of his final autobiography.

17. Martin, *The Mind of Frederick Douglass*, 256–57.

18. *The Liberator*, January 18, 1856.

19. *North Star*, August 24, 1849; Yee, *Black Women Abolitionists*, 45.

20. Yee, *Black Women Abolitionists*, 8.

21. Yee, *Black Women Abolitionists*, 40; Ernest, "Motherhood Beyond the Gate," 182–85; Welter, "The Cult of True Womanhood: 1820–1860," 152.

22. Welter, "The Cult of True Womanhood, 1820–1860"; Yee, *Black Women Abolitionists*, 40–41; Carby, *Reconstructing Womanhood*, 49.

23. Yee, *Black Women Abolitionists*, 89, notes that the original constitution for the Female Anti-Slavery Society of Salem emphasized black community development as the primary objective rather than the abolition of slavery.

24. Yee, *Black Women Abolitionists*, 91; *The Liberator*, February 28, 1839, 21.

25. Jacobs, *Incidents in the Life of a Slave Girl*, 1. All subsequent references to the text appear parenthetically as *I*.

26. Robyn Warhol makes a strong case for distinguishing between what she calls an "engaging narrator" and a "distancing narrator": "[T]he 'feminine' *engaging* narrator—who employs direct address to an extra-textual narratee in order to reinforce realism and to encourage the actual reader's emotional engagement with the fictional action—and the 'masculine' *distancing* narrator—who addresses a fictive narratee for metafictional effect, indeed to subvert realism and draw the actual reader's attention to the constructedness of the text" (" 'Reader, Can You Imagine? No, You Cannot,' " 59).

27. Yellin, in her Introduction to Jacobs, *Incidents in the Life of a Slave Girl*, vii.

28. Blassingame, *The Slave Community*, 373. See also Goldsby, " 'I Disguised My Hand,' " 13.

29. Warhol, " 'Reader, Can You Imagine? No, You Cannot,' " 63.

30. Jacobs, *Incidents in the Life of a Slave Girl*, 232.

31. Goldsby, " 'I Disguised My Hand,' " 17–19.

32. Peterson, "*Doers of the Word*," 192.

33. Peterson, "*Doers of the Word*," 192.

34. Warhol, " 'Reader, Can You Imagine? No, You Cannot,' " 62; Smith, "Resisting the Gaze of Embodiment," 75–110.

35. Gunning, "Reading and Redemption in *Incidents in the Life of a Slave Girl*," 134–37.

36. Smith, "Resisting the Gaze of Embodiment," 99.

37. Carby, *Reconstructing Womanhood*, 49.

38. Gunning, "Reading and Redemption in *Incidents in the Life of a Slave Girl*," 139–42.

39. Andrews, *To Tell a Free Story*, 167–79, 247–48.

40. Ernest, "Motherhood Beyond the Gate," 194–95.

CHAPTER 5
THE RECONSTRUCTION OF RACE IN WILLIAM AND ELLEN CRAFT'S
RUNNING A THOUSAND MILES FOR FREEDOM

1. Aanerud, "Fictions of Whiteness: Speaking the Names of Whiteness in U.S. Literature," 35–38; Ferguson, Gever, Minh-ha, and West, *Out There*, 9–14; Frankenberg, *White Women, Race Matters*, 1–22, 191–235; Frankenberg, " 'When We Are Capable of Stopping, We Begin to See,' " 3–17; Allen, *The Invention of the White Race*, 1–24, 27–51.

2. Morrison, *Playing in the Dark*, xii; hooks, *Black Looks*, 165–78.

3. Du Bois, *The Souls of Black Folk*; Ellison, *Invisible Man*; Gilroy, *The Black Atlantic*, 1–40.

4. hooks, *Black Looks*, 165–78.

5. Holt, "Marking," 1–20.

6. Craft, *Running a Thousand Miles for Freedom*, iv. All subsequent references to the text appear parenthetically as *RTMF*.

7. Robinson, "It Takes One to Know One," 721–22.

8. Haney Lopez, *White by Law*, 1–3, 111–53.

9. Kawash, "The Autobiography of an Ex-Coloured Man," 70–73.

10. Du Bois, *The Souls of Black Folk*, 39; Johnson, *A World of Difference*, 166.

11. Thompson, "Time Traveling and Border Crossing," 93–109; Twine, Warren, and Ferrandiz, *Just Black? Multiracial Identity* (video).

12. Wray and Newitz, eds., *White Trash*, 1–12.

13. Weinauer, " 'A Most Respectable Looking Gentleman,' " 47–53; Garber, *Vested Interests*, 281–85.

14. Weinauer, " 'A Most Respectable Looking Gentleman,' " 37–53.

15. Morrison, *Playing in the Dark*, 5.

Epilogue
Caliban's Reprise

1. Williams, *The Alchemy of Race and Rights*, 46.

2. Taylor, "Voices from the Veil," 342; Sisko, " 'Writing in the Spaces Left,' " 196–97.

3. hooks, *Black Looks*, 13.

4. hooks and West, *Breaking Bread*, 87.

BIBLIOGRAPHY

Aanerud, Rebecca. "Fictions of Whiteness: Speaking the Names of Whiteness in U.S. Literature." In *Displacing Whiteness: Essays in Social and Cultural Criticism*, edited by Ruth Frankenberg, 35–59. Durham, N.C.: Duke University Press, 1997.

Abzug, Robert H. "The Influence of Garrisonian Abolitionists' Fears of Slave Violence on the Antislavery Argument, 1829–40." *Journal of Negro History* 55 (1970): 15–28.

Allen, Theodore W. *The Invention of the White Race. Vol. 1: Racial Oppression and Social Control.* London: Verso, 1994.

Andrews, William L. "Inter(racial)textuality in Nineteenth-Century Southern Narrative." In *Influence and Intertextuality in Literary History*, edited by Jay Clayton and Eric Rothstein, 298–317. Madison: University of Wisconsin Press, 1991.

———. *To Tell a Free Story: The First Century of Afro-American Autobiography, 1760–1865.* Urbana: University of Illinois Press, 1986.

Aptheker, Herbert. *Abolitionism: A Revolutionary Movement.* Boston: Twayne Publishers, 1989.

———. *American Negro Slave Revolts.* New York: International Publishers, 1983.

———. *Nat Turner's Slave Rebellion.* New York: Humanities Press, 1966.

Awkward, Michael. *Inspiriting Influences: Tradition, Revision, and Afro-American Women's Novels.* New York: Columbia University Press, 1987.

Baker, Jr. Houston A. "Autobiographical Acts and the Voice of the Southern Slave." In *Critical Essays on Frederick Douglass*, edited by William L. Andrews, 94–107. Boston: G. K. Hall and Co., 1991.

———. *Blues, Ideology, and Afro-American Literature: A Vernacular Theory.* Chicago: University of Chicago Press, 1984.

———. *Long Black Song: Essays in Black American Literature and Culture.* Charlottesville: University of Virginia Press, 1972.

———. *Modernism and the Harlem Renaissance.* Chicago: University of Chicago Press, 1987.

———. *Singers of Daybreak: Studies in Black American Literature.* Washington, D.C.: Howard University Press, 1974.

Bakhtin, Mikhail. "Discourse in the Novel." In *The Dialogic Imagination: Four Essays by Mikhail Bakhtin*, edited by Michael Holquist, translated by Caryl Emerson and Michael Holquist, 259–422. Austin: University of Texas Press, 1981.

Barnes, Gilbert H. and Dwight L. Dumond. *The Letters of Theodore Dwight Weld, Angelina Grinke Weld, and Sarah Grimke.* 2 vols. New York: Appleton, 1943.

Blassingame, John W. "Using the Testimony of Ex-Slaves: Approaches and Problems." In *The Slave's Narrative*, edited by Charles T. Davis and Henry Louis Gates, Jr., 78–98. New York: Oxford University Press, 1985.

———. *The Slave Community.* New York: Oxford University Press, 1979.

Braxton, Joanne. *Black Women Writing Autobiography: A Tradition within a Tradition*. Philadelphia: Temple University Press, 1989.

Brotz, Howard, ed. *Negro Social and Political Thought 1850–1920*. New York: Basic Books, 1966.

Butler-Evans, Elliot. *Race, Gender, and Desire: Narrative Strategies in the Fiction of Toni Cade Bambara, Toni Morrison, and Alice Walker*. Philadelphia: Temple University Press, 1989.

Callahan, John F. *In the African American Grain: Call-and-Response in Twentieth-Century Black Fiction*. Middletown, Conn.: Wesleyan University Press, 1988.

Carby, Hazel. *Reconstructing Womanhood: The Emergence of the Afro-American Woman Novelist*. New York: Oxford University Press, 1987.

Carson, Sharon. "Shaking the Foundation: Liberation Theology in *Narrative of the Life of Frederick Douglass*." *Religion and Literature* 24 (Summer 1992): 19–34.

Cheyfitz, Eric. *The Poetics of Imperialism: Translation and Colonization from* The Tempest *to* Tarzan. New York: Oxford University Press, 1991.

Costanzo, Angelo. *Surprizing Narrative: Olaudah Equiano and the Beginnings of Black Autobiography*. Westport, Conn.: Greenwood Press, 1987.

Cox, James M. "Autobiography and America." *The Virginia Quarterly Review* 47 (1971): 252–77.

Craft, William and Ellen. *Running a Thousand Miles for Freedom*. New York: Arno, 1969.

Davidson, Cathy N. *Revolution and the Word: The Rise of the Novel in America*. New York: Oxford University Press, 1986.

Demos, John. "The Antislavery Movement and the Problem of Violent 'Means.' " *The New England Quarterly* 37 (December 1964): 501–26.

Dorsey, Peter A. "Becoming the Other: The Mimesis of Metaphor in Douglass's *My Bondage and My Freedom*." *PMLA* 111 (May 1996): 435–50.

Douglass, Frederick. *My Bondage and My Freedom*. In *Autobiographies*, 103–452. New York: The Library of America, 1994.

———. *Narrative of the Life of Frederick Douglass, an American Slave*. In *Autobiographies*, 1–102. New York: The Library of America, 1994.

Du Bois, W.E.B. *The Souls of Black Folk*. Edited and with an introduction by David W. Blight and Robert Gooding-Williams. Boston: Bedford Books, 1997.

During, Simon. "Postmodernism or Postcolonialism?" *Landfall* 39 (1985): 366–80.

Elkins, Stanley M. *Slavery: A Problem in American Institutional and Intellectual Life*. New York: The Universal Library, 1963.

Ellison, Ralph. "Blues People." In *The Collected Essays of Ralph Ellison*. Edited and with an introduction by John F. Callahan, 278–87. New York: The Modern Library, 1995.

———. *Invisible Man*. New York: Vintage Books, 1995.

Ernest, John. "Motherhood Beyond the Gate: Jacobs's Epistemic Challenge in *Incidents in the Life of a Slave Girl*." In *Harriet Jacobs and* Incidents in the Life of a

Slave Girl, edited by Deborah M. Garfield and Rafia Zafar, 179–98. New York: Cambridge University Press, 1996.

Fabricant, Daniel S. "Thomas R. Gray and William Styron: Finally, A Critical Look at the 1831 *Confessions of Nat Turner.*" *American Journal of Legal History* 37 (1993): 332–61.

Faulkner, William. *Light in August*. New York: Vintage, 1990.

Felman, Shoshana. *What Does a Woman Want?: Reading and Sexual Difference*. Baltimore: Johns Hopkins University Press, 1993.

——— and Dori Laub. *Testimony: Crisis of Witnessing in Literature, Psychoanalysis, and History*. New York and London: Routledge, 1992.

Ferguson, Russell, Martha Gever, Trinh T. Minh-ha, and Cornel West, eds. *Out There: Marginality and Contemporary Cultures*. New York: The New Museum of Contemporary Art, 1990.

Fisk Collection. *Unwritten History of Slavery: Autobiographical Accounts of Negro Ex-Slaves*. Nashville: Social Science Institute, Fisk University, 1945.

Foster, Frances Smith. "Neither Auction Block nor Pedestal: 'The Life and Religious Experiences of Jarena Lee, a Coloured Lady.' " In *The Female Autograph*, edited by Domna C. Stanton, 143–69. New York: New York Literary Forum, 1984.

———. *Witnessing Slavery: The Development of Ante-Bellum Slave Narratives*. Westport, Conn.: Greenwood Press, 1979.

Frankenberg, Ruth. " 'When We Are Capable of Stopping, We Begin to See': Being White, Seeing Whiteness." In *Names We Call Home: Autobiography on Racial Identity*, edited by Becky Thompson and Sangeeta Tyagi, 3–17. New York: Routledge, 1996.

———. *White Women, Race Matters: The Social Construction of Whiteness*. Minneapolis: University of Minnesota Press, 1993.

Fredrickson, George M. *The Black Image in the White Mind: The Debate on Afro-American Character and Destiny, 1817–1914*. New York: Harper and Row, 1971.

Garber, Marjorie. *Vested Interests: Cross-dressing and Cultural Anxiety*. New York: Routledge, 1992.

Garrison, W. P. and F. J. *William Lloyd Garrison 1805–1879: The Story of His Life as Told by His Children*. 4 vols. New York: The Century Co., 1885–89.

Gates, Jr., Henry Louis. "Binary Oppositions in Chapter One of *Narrative of the Life of Frederick Douglass an American Slave Written by Himself.*" In *Critical Essays on Frederick Douglass*, edited by William L. Andrews, 79–93. Boston: G. K. Hall, 1991.

———. *Figures in Black: Words, Signs, and the "Racial" Self*. New York: Oxford University Press, 1987.

———. *The Signifying Monkey: A Theory of Afro-American Literary Criticism*. New York: Oxford University Press, 1988.

———. *Six Women's Slave Narratives*. New York: Oxford University Press, 1988.

Gayle, Jr., Addison. *The Way of the New World: The Black Novel in America*. Garden City, N.Y.: Anchor Press/Doubleday, 1975.

Genovese, Eugene D. *Roll, Jordan, Roll: The World the Slaves Made*. New York: Random House, 1972.

Gibson, Donald B. "Faith, Doubt, and Apostasy: Evidence of Things Unseen in Frederick Douglass's *Narrative*." In *Frederick Douglass: New Literary and Historical Essays*, edited by Eric J. Sundquist, 84–98. New York: Cambridge University Press, 1991.

———. *The Politics of Literary Expression: A Study of Major Black Writers*. Westport, Conn.: Greenwood Press, 1981.

Gilroy, Paul. *The Black Atlantic: Modernity and Double Consciousness*. Cambridge, Mass.: Harvard University Press, 1993.

Goddu, Teresa A. and Craig V. Smith. "Scenes of Writing in Frederick Douglass's *Narrative*: Autobiography and the Creation of Self." *The Southern Review* 25 (Autumn): 822–40.

Goldsby, Jacqueline. " 'I Disguised My Hand:' Writing Versions of the Truth in Harriet Jacobs's *Incidents in the Life of a Slave Girl* and John Jacobs's 'A True Tale of Slavery.' " In *Harriet Jacobs and* Incidents in the Life of a Slave Girl: *New Critical Essays*, edited by Deborah M. Garfield and Rafia Zafar, 11–43. New York: Cambridge University Press, 1996.

Graham, George R. "Black Letters; or Uncle Tom Foolery in Literature." *Graham's Illustrated Magazine of Literature, Romance, Art, and Fashion* 42 (February 1853): 209–15.

Greenblatt, Stephen. *Renaissance Self-Fashioning: From More to Shakespeare*. Chicago: University of Chicago Press, 1980.

Grimke, Angelina. *The Letters of Theodore Dwight Weld, Angelina Grimke Weld, and Sarah Grimke*. Edited by Gilbert H. Barnes and Dwight L. Dumond. 2 vols. New York: Appleton, 1943.

Gunning, Sandra. "Reading and Redemption in *Incidents in the Life of a Slave Girl*." In *Harriet Jacobs and* Incidents in the Life of a Slave Girl: *New Critical Essays*, edited by Deborah M. Garfield and Rafia Zafar, 131–55. New York: Cambridge University Press, 1996.

Gutman, Herbert G. *The Black Family in Slavery and Freedom, 1750–1925*. New York: Pantheon Books, 1976.

Hale, Dorothy J. "Bakhtin in African American Literary Theory." *ELH* 61 (Summer 1994): 445–71.

Hall, Stuart. "Cultural Identity and Diaspora." In *Identity: Community, Culture, Difference*, edited by Jonathan Rutherford, 222–37. London: Lawrence & Wishart, 1990.

Haney Lopez, Ian F. *White by Law: The Legal Construction of Race*. New York: New York University Press, 1996.

Hawley, John C. "We Wretched of the Earth: The Search for a Language of Justice." In *Postcolonial Literature and the Biblical Call for Justice*, edited by Susan VanZanten Gallagher, 125–35. Jackson: University Press of Mississippi, 1994.

Hedin, Raymond. "The American Slave Narrative: The Justification of the Picaro." *American Literature* 53 (January 1982): 630–45.

———. "Probable Readers, Possible Stories: The Limits of Nineteenth-Century Black Narrative." In *Readers in History: Nineteenth-Century American Literature and the Contexts of Response,* edited by James I. Machor, 180–205. Baltimore: Johns Hopkins University Press, 1993.

Holt, Thomas C. "Marking: Race, Race-Making, and the Writing of History." *American Historical Review* 100 (February 1995): 1–20

hooks, bell. *Black Looks: Race and Representation.* Boston: South End Press, 1992.

——— and Cornell West. *Breaking Bread: Insurgent Black Intellectual Life.* Boston: South End Press, 1991.

Huggins, Nathan Irvin. *Harlem Renaissance.* New York: Oxford University Press, 1971.

Hurston, Zora Neale. "Characteristics of Negro Expression." In *Negro: An Anthology,* edited by Nancy Cunard, 24–31; rpt., abridged ed., edited by Hugh Ford. New York: Frederick Ungar Publishing Co., Inc., 1970.

Jacobs, Harriet A. [Linda Brent]. *Incidents in the Life of a Slave Girl.* Edited by Jean Fagan Yellin. Cambridge, Mass.: Harvard University Press, 1987.

Jakobson, Roman and Morris Hale. *Fundamentals of Language.* The Hague: Mouton, 1971.

Jameson, Frederic. *The Prison-House of Language: A Critical Account of Structuralism and Russian Formalism.* Princeton, N.J.: Princeton University Press, 1972.

Johnson, Barbara. *A World of Difference.* Baltimore: Johns Hopkins University Press, 1987.

Jones, Gayl. *Liberating Voices: Oral Tradition in African American Literature.* Cambridge, Mass.: Harvard University Press, 1991.

Kawash, Samira. "The Autobiography of an Ex-Coloured Man: (Passing For) Black Passing for White." In *Passing and the Fictions of Identity,* edited by Elaine K. Ginsberg, 59–74. Durham, N.C.: Duke University Press, 1996.

Kazin, Alfred. "Autobiography as Narrative." *The Michigan Quarterly Review* 3 (1964): 210–16.

Kibbey, Ann. "Language in Slavery." In *Frederick Douglass's* Narrative of the Life of Frederick Douglass, edited and with an introduction by Harold Bloom, 131–52. New York: Chelsea House Publishers, 1988.

——— and Michele Stepto. "The Antilanguage of Slavery: Frederick Douglass's 1845 *Narrative.*" In *Critical Essays on Frederick Douglass,* edited by William L. Andrews, 166–91. Boston: G. K. Hall and Co., 1991.

Levi-Strauss, Claude. *Totemism.* New York: Penguin, 1969.

Levine, Lawrence W. *Black Culture and Black Consciousness: Afro-American Folk Thought from Slavery to Freedom.* New York: Oxford University Press, 1977.

Liberator, The. Edited by William Lloyd Garrison. Ann Arbor, Mich.: University Microfilms. American Periodical Series, Jan. 1, 1831-Dec. 29, 1865. Reels 391–99. Microfilm.

Lorde, Audre. "The Master's Tools Will Never Dismantle the Master's House." In *Sister Outsider: Essays and Speeches by Audre Lorde*, 110–13. Freedom, Ca.: The Crossing Press, 1984.

Major, Clarence, ed. *Juba to Jive: The Dictionary of African-American Slang*. New York: Viking, 1994.

Marcus, Laura. "Theories of Autobiography." In *The Uses of Autobiography*, edited by Julia Swindells, 13–23. London: Taylor and Francis, 1995.

Martin, Waldo. *The Mind of Frederick Douglass*. Chapel Hill: University of North Carolina Press, 1984.

Morrison, Toni. *Playing in the Dark: Whiteness and the Literary Imagination*. Cambridge, Mass.: Harvard University Press, 1992.

———, ed. *Race-ing Justice, En-gendering Power: Essays on Anita Hill, Clarence Thomas, and the Construction of Social Reality*. New York: Pantheon Books, 1992.

———. "Unspeakable Things Unspoken: The Afro-American Presence in American Literature." *Michigan Quarterly Review* 28 (Winter 1989): 1–34.

Moses, Wilson J. "Writing Freely?: Frederick Douglass and the Constraints of Recialized Writing." In *Frederick Douglas: New Literary and Historical Essays*, edited by Eric J. Sundquist, 66–83. New York: Cambridge University Press, 1991.

Niemtzow, Annette. "The Problematic Self in Autobiography: The Example of the Slave Narrative." In *The Art of Slave Narrative*, edited by John Sekora and Darwin T. Turner, 96–109. Macomb, Ill.: Western Illinois University, 1982.

Ngũgĩ, wa Thiong'o. *Moving the Centre: The Struggle for Cultural Freedoms*. London: J. Currey, 1993.

Oates, Stephen B. *The Fires of Jubilee: Nat Turner's Fierce Rebellion*. New York: Harper & Row, 1975.

Olney, James. " 'I Was Born': Slave Narratives, Their Status as Autobiography and as Literature." In *The Slave's Narrative*, edited by Charles T. Davis and Henry Louis Gates, Jr., 148–75. New York: Oxford University Press, 1985.

O'Meally, Robert. "The Text Was Meant to Be Preached." In *Frederick Douglass's Narrative of the Life of Frederick Douglass*, edited and with an introduction by Harold Bloom, 77–94. New York: Chelsea House Publishers, 1988.

Pascal, Roy. *Design and Truth in Autobiography*. London: Routledge, 1960.

Peterson, Carla L. *"Doers of the Word": African-American Women Speakers and Writers in the North (1830–1880)*. New York: Oxford University Press, 1995.

Phillips, Ulrich Bonnell. *American Negro Slavery: A Survey of the Supply, Employment and Control of Negro Labor as Determined by the Plantation Regime*. New York: D. Appleton-Century Company, 1918, rpt. 1940.

Rawick, George P. *From Sundown to Sunup: The Making of the Black Community*. The American Slave: A Composite Autobiography, vol 1. Contributions in Afro-American and African Studies, no. 11. Westport, Conn.: Greenwood Press, 1972.

Renza, Louis A. "The Veto of the Imagination: A Theory of Autobiography." In *Autobiography: Essays Theoretical and Critical*, edited by James Olney, 268–95. Princeton, N.J.: Princeton University Press, 1980.

Ring, Betty J. " 'Painting by Numbers': Figuring Frederick Douglass." In *The Discourse of Slavery: Aphra Behn to Toni Morrison*, edited by Carl Plasa and Betty J. Ring, 118–43. London: Routledge, 1994.

Robbins, Sarah. "Gendering the History of the Antislavery Narrative: Juxtaposing *Uncle Tom's Cabin* and *Benito Cereno, Beloved*, and *Middle Passage*." *American Quarterly* 49 (September 1997): 531–73.

Robinson, Amy. "It Takes One to Know One: Passing and Communities of Common Interest." *Critical Inquiry* 20 (Summer 1994): 715–36.

Roper, Moses. *A Narrative of the Adventures and Escape of Moses Roper from American Slavery; with a preface by The Rev. T. Price, D.D.* New York: Negro Universities Press, 1970.

Rowe, John Carlos. "Between Politics and Poetics: Frederick Douglass and Postmodernity." In *Reconstructing American Literary and Historical Studies*, edited by Gunther H. Lenz, Harmut Keil, and Sabine Brock-Sallah, 192–210. Frankfurt: Campus Verlag, 1990.

Sekora, John. " 'Mr. Editor, If You Please': Frederick Douglass, *My Bondage and My Freedom*, and the End of the Abolitionist Imprint." *Calloloo* 17.2 (1994) 608–26.

Shakespeare, William. *The Tempest*. In *The Complete Signet Classic Shakespeare*, edited by Sylvan Barnet, 1537–68. New York: Harcourt Brace Jovanovich, Inc., 1972.

Sisco, Lisa. " 'Writing in the Spaces Left': Literacy as a Process of Becoming in the Narratives of Frederick Douglass." *American Transcendental Quarterly* 9 (September 1995): 195–227.

Smith, Sidonie. "Resisting the Gaze of Embodiment: Women's Autobiography in the Nineteenth Century." In *American Women's Autobiography: Fea(s)ts of Memory*, edited by Margo Culley, 75–110. Madison: University of Wisconsin Press, 1992.

Smith, Valerie. *Self-Discovery and Authority in Afro-American Narrative*. Cambridge, Mass.: Harvard University Press, 1987.

Stampp, Kenneth M. *The Peculiar Institution: Slavery in the Ante-Bellum South*. New York: Alfred A. Knopf, 1956, rpt. 1963.

Starling, Marion Wilson. *The Slave Narrative: Its Place in American History*, second edition. Washington, D.C.: Howard University Press, 1988.

Stepto, Robert B. *From Behind the Veil: A Study of Afro-American Narrative*. Urbana: University of Illinois Press, 1979.

Stowe, Harriet Beecher. *Uncle Tom's Cabin*. Edited by Elizabeth Ammons. New York: W.W. Norton and Company, 1994.

Sundquist, Eric J. *To Wake the Nations: Race in the Making of American Literature*. Cambridge, Mass.: The Belknap Press of Harvard University Press, 1993.

Taylor, Gordon O. "Voices from the Veil: Black American Autobiography." *The Georgia Review* 35 (Summer 1981): 341–61.

Thompson, Becky. "Time Traveling and Border Crossing: Reflections on White Identity." In *Names We Call Home: Autobiography on Racial Identity*, edited by Becky Thompson and Sangeeta Tyagi, 93–109. New York: Routledge, 1996.

Tragle, Henry Irving. *The Southampton Slave Revolt of 1831: A Compilation of Source Material*. Amherst: University of Massachusetts Press, 1966.

Turner, Nat. *The Confessions of Nat Turner and Related Documents*. Edited by Kenneth S. Greenberg. Boston: Bedford Books of St. Martin's Press, 1996.

Twine, France Winddance, Jonathan W. Warren, and Francisco Ferrandiz. *Just Black? Multiracial Identity* (video). New York: Filmmakers Library, 1991.

Van Leer, David. "Reading Slavery: The Anxiety of Ethnicity in Douglass's *Narrative*." In *Frederick Douglass: New Literary and Historical Essays*, edited by Eric J. Sundquist, 118–40. New York: Cambridge University Press, 1991.

Warhol, Robyn R. " 'Reader, Can You Imagine? No, You Cannot: The Narratee as Other in Harriet Jacobs's Text.' " *Narrative* 3 (January 1995): 57–72.

Weinauer, Ellen M. " 'A Most Respectable Looking Gentleman': Passing, Possession, and Transgression in *Running a Thousand Miles for Freedom*. In *Passing and the Fictions of Identity*, edited by Elaine K. Ginsberg, 37–56. Durham, N.C.: Duke University Press, 1996.

Welter, Barbara J. "The Cult of True Womanhood, 1820–1860." *American Quarterly* 18 (Summer 1966): 151–74.

Williams, Patricia. *The Alchemy of Race and Rights: Diary of a Law Professor*. Cambridge, Mass.: Harvard University Press, 1991.

Wray, Matt, and Annalee Newitz, eds. *White Trash: Race and Class in America*. New York: Routledge, 1997.

Wright, Richard. *12 Million Black Voices: A Folk History of the Negro in the United States*. New York: Viking Press, 1941. Reprint New York: Thunders Mouth's Press, 1988.

Yee, Shirley J. *Black Women Abolitionists: A Study in Activism, 1828–1860*. Knoxville: University of Tennessee Press, 1992.

Ziolkowski, Thad. "Antithesis: The Dialectic of Violence and Literacy in Frederick Douglass's *Narrative* of 1845." In *Critical Essays on Frederick Douglass*, edited by William L. Andrews, 148–65. Boston: G. K. Hall and Co., 1991.

INDEX

About the Author

STERLING LECATER BLAND, JR. is Assistant Professor of English at Rutgers University.

Recent Titles in
Contributions in Afro-American and African Studies

New Trends and Developments in African Religions
Peter B. Clarke, editor

Black Women Writers and the American Neo-Slave Narrative: Femininity Unfettered
Elizabeth Ann Beaulieu

African Settings in Contemporary American Novels
Dave Kuhne

The Harlem Renaissance: The One and the Many
Mark Helbling

Willis Richardson, Forgotten Pioneer of African-American Drama
Christine Rauchfuss Gray

Critical Essays on Alice Walker
Ikenna Dieke, editor

Education and Independence: Education in South Africa, 1658–1988
Simphiwe A. Hlatshwayo

African American Autobiography and the Quest for Freedom
Roland L. Williams, Jr.

The White Image in the Black Mind: A Study of African American Literature
Jane Davis

Black Leadership for Social Change
Jacob U. Gordon

Mythatypes: Signatures and Signs of African/Diaspora and Black Goddesses
Alexis Brooks De Vita

African Visions: Literary Images, Political Change, and Social Struggle in
Contemporary Africa
Cheryl B. Mwaria, Silvia Federici, and Joseph McLaren, editors